THE DOMINICAN REPUBLIC

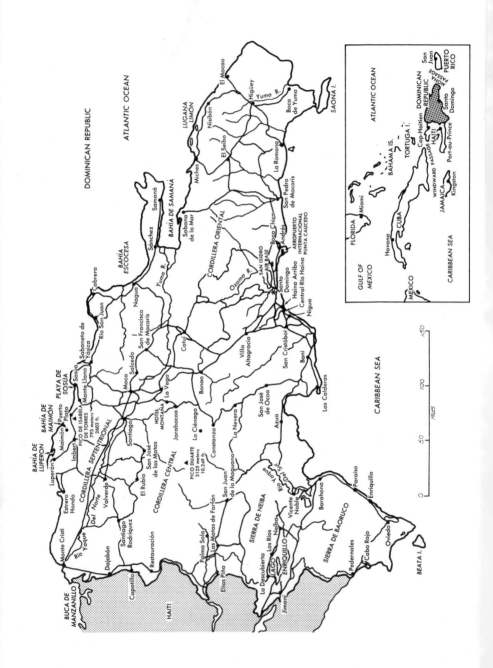

THE DOMINICAN REPUBLIC

NATION IN TRANSITION

Howard J. Wiarda

FREDERICK A. PRAEGER, *Publishers*

New York • Washington • London

FREDERICK A. PRAEGER, PUBLISHERS
111 Fourth Avenue, New York, N.Y. 10003, U.S.A.
5, Cromwell Place, London S.W. 7, England

Published in the United States of America in 1969
by Frederick A. Praeger, Inc., Publishers

© 1969 by Frederick A. Praeger, Inc.

Library of Congress Catalog Card Number: 69-12717

Printed in the United States of America

To
Kristy Lynn Wiarda
our *dominicana*

PREFACE

FOR SOME TIME there has been a felt need for a general book about the Dominican Republic. To this writer's knowledge, there is no single volume which provides the general reader with an integrated introduction to the geography, history, society, culture, economy, and politics of this Caribbean nation or which is oriented toward the theme of national development and modernization. This book has been written to help fill the void in our knowledge of what has become a crucial and important country.

Though the book was written for the general reader—the college student, the public official, the Peace Corps volunteer, the person who has acquired an interest in Dominican affairs—it is hoped that the specialist may find it of interest as well. And though an attempt has been made to avoid as much as possible the use of footnotes and unexplained professional jargon, this is not to say that the book is without seriousness or scholarship. It is part of a long-term project dealing with social change and political development in the Dominican Republic and represents this writer's preliminary assessment—after some six years of studying, living in, and reading and writing about the country—of the complex problems and issues involved in the modernization process.

Anyone doing research on or writing about the Dominican Republic is immediately struck by the scarcity of good basic studies on almost all aspects of the country. There is as yet no core of basic data upon which to build. It is for this reason that a book such as the present one, which aims within a broad and all-encompassing framework to present a wide-ranging picture of what is an increasingly complex country, must be modestly offered not as the whole truth but as a study based on the information currently available. Because our understanding of the Dominican system is still so limited, the statements made and conclusions reached in this volume must be considered tentative and subject to revision. It is hoped, however, that some of the ideas expressed in the book may stimulate others to explore them more closely and to help build up the solid foundation of hard, empirical knowledge concerning the Dominican Republic which is so sorely lacking.

In the course of studying the Dominican polity, this writer has become indebted to so many people who have contributed to his understanding of the country that it is impossible to begin to mention them all. Special thanks for assistance in the preparation of this particular volume, however, are due to Abraham F. Lowenthal of Harvard University, Víctor Alba, and Iêda Siqueira Wiarda—all of whom have read and offered helpful comments on the manuscript. Whatever errors of fact or interpretation remain, however, are solely the responsibility of the author.

H. J. W.

Amherst, Massachusetts

CONTENTS

A section of photographs follows page 122.

THE DOMINICAN REPUBLIC

Chapter I

INTRODUCTION

THE DOMINICAN REPUBLIC has in recent years achieved an importance out of all proportion to its size or population. The dictatorship of Generalissimo Rafael Trujillo, who ruled the country with an iron fist from 1930 until his assassination in 1961, achieved the dubious distinction of being perhaps the most ruthless and absolute—and certainly the longest-lived—tyranny in Latin America in the twentieth century. Following Trujillo's death, a vigorous attempt, with enormous United States aid and backing, was made to convert the Dominican Republic—only a short way from Communist Cuba—into a showcase of democratic development which would offer Latin America a model of how to achieve much-needed reform without resort to the totalitarian methods of Castroism.

This attempt ended in inglorious failure when the democratic and constitutional government that the Dominicans and the United States had worked so hard to establish was overthrown after only seven months in office by a small clique of *status quo*–oriented businessmen, politicians, Church officials, and military officers. The pressures that had built up in the country as a result of the frustration of democratic development culminated in 1965 in revolution, civil war, and United States military intervention, leaving the Dominican Republic with a bitter legacy and in a disintegrated state from which it has only recently begun to recover. All of these fast-moving events—dictatorship, assassination, democracy, *coup d'état*, revolution, civil war, U.S. inter-

3

vention—focused world-wide attention on this Caribbean nation.

Instability and revolutionary changes in the Dominican Republic are symptomatic of the profound transformations presently taking place in many areas of the globe. With more than 120 years of independent life behind it, the Dominican Republic can hardly be considered a "new nation"; yet, it shares with the newer nations of Africa, Asia, and the Middle East many of the same problems and dilemmas of development and modernization. The Dominican Republic, like these others, is currently experiencing a delayed industrial-technological-scientific-modernizing revolution which finds concomitant expression in the demands of its people for a better life, social justice, a more democratic political system, a greater share in national decision-making, and a more equitable division of the wealth of the land. These new demands are popularly referred to as the "revolution of rising expectations"—the impatient desire on the part of the peoples of less developed countries to leap into the modern era and share in its benefits without waiting the decades or even centuries which it took the more developed nations to evolve into modern, industrialized, wealthy, democratic states. As the case of the Dominican Republic illustrates, these broad changes and revolutionary demands raise many difficult questions not only for the countries involved in the modernization process but also for U.S. foreign policy.

Like many nations of Latin America, Asia, and Africa, the Dominican Republic is in many ways poor, backward, and underdeveloped. Most Dominicans have not yet begun to share in the benefits that have come from the accelerated economic and technological improvements of recent decades. While the small Dominican elite and small middle class of the capital city live in a manner not very different from that of their counterparts in economically more advanced nations, this wealth has not yet begun to trickle down into the lower ranks of the society; most of the population still lives in abysmal and grinding poverty

—without adequate food, clothing, housing, health care, educational opportunities, and, above all, without hope of ever achieving anything better.

The Dominican Republic is also plagued by a rigid, hierarchical class and caste system with a few, lighter-skinned elements at the top enjoying most of the wealth and power and the many darker-skinned people at the bottom having almost nothing at all. Social mobility is extremely limited; there are few Horatio Algers in the Dominican Republic, and only rarely does someone from one social sector succeed in achieving a higher level. Most Dominicans are born and raised, marry and die at the same social level as their parents; the chances for improving one's lot are almost nil. Though it is presently beginning to change, the Dominican social structure remains in many respects semifeudal, with a small elite at the upper levels, a large bulk at the lower levels, and relatively few in between.

The Dominican Republic's 3.5 million long-suffering people have never had much experience with stable, democratic, self-government. The smallness and powerlessness of the nation, coupled with its strategic location, have frequently made it the prey of foreign powers. The Dominicans have had more revolutions, more civil wars, and more constitutions than all but a few countries in the world; and they have been ruled by some of the most bloodthirsty tyrants ever to come to power anywhere. Never have the Dominicans enjoyed more than fleeting periods of peace and order, combined with liberty and freedom. Even today, the fundamental premises of their constitution—that government should be "civil, republican, democratic, and representative"—are still ideals and not fully operating principles in the country.

Though industry and manufacturing have expanded in recent decades, the Dominican Republic is still essentially a rural-agricultural and not an urban-industrial society. A very few people own most of the land, and most of the population has no or insufficient land. Basic foodstuffs are scarce, and malnutrition and starvation are prevalent. Were it not for the fact that its chief crop is sugar cane, the Dominican Republic—at least until recently—would have resembled in some ways the stereotype of the sleepy, poverty-ridden "banana republic." Now, however, this picture, too, is rapidly changing; the Dominican people have "woken up" and have begun to acquire wants and demands of revolutionary proportions.

The Dominican Republic has few of the prerequisites deemed necessary for the establishment of a stable, functioning, democratic system. Illiteracy is widespread, and the communications and transportation networks are not adequate for the country's needs. Few of the groups by which the different sectors of the population can make their voices heard—interest associations, political parties, etc.—are well organized or efficiently led; and government and politics are largely the monopoly of the few. Nepotism and corruption are rampant in many areas of public life, and an absolutist, authoritarian tradition, traceable to the early Spanish colonial system, still dominates in the political life of the nation. For many years, political authority was largely determined by the interplay of rival elite families whose ideologies or programs did not differ significantly, and civil war or revolution was the means for effecting changes of regimes. Rival *caudillos* (men on horseback), often at the service of the "first families," jockeyed to gain the favor of rag-tag unprofessional bands of armed camp followers, and they galloped in and out of the presidential palace with regularity.

The traditional, semifeudal structure of Dominican society and political life, based upon hierarchy, strict class rank, family favoritism, caudilloism, and authoritarianism, remained by and large intact as the country entered the present century. But in more recent decades the entire system—economic, social, ideological, and political—began to change at an ever accelerating speed. As the old order started to give way, newer concepts and institutions began to replace it—and the Dominican Republic, slowly, uncertainly, but probably irreversibly, began the great process of transformation from traditional to more modern, twentieth-century ways.

The traditional structure started to crumble for a variety of reasons. Ideas that were new to the Dominican Republic—democracy, Marxism, liberalism, capitalism, positivism, socialism—competed in offering men new ways to organize their society and institutions. The first stirrings of industrialization and over-all economic growth gave rise to new groups with values that were not always compatible with the old order. Thus, the traditionally silent, unorganized, and unrepresented peasant was lured to the sugar mills and the cities by the promise of a job and hence of a better life; and it was not long before an organized labor movement began to demand a say in national affairs. A new business-commercial-manufacturing elite began to challenge the position of the older landed elite. The civil service and the armed forces were enlarged, expanded, and professionalized, and they also began to play a more important role in national affairs. A variety of new middle-class elements—technicians, clerks, small businessmen, managers, professionals, military officers, government workers, etc.—took their place in Dominican society. The insistent demands for improved living standards on the part of many sectors of the population reached such an intensity that they could no longer be ignored. New ideas, changing values, economic stimulation, and broad societal changes combined in a way that challenged and eventually began to break down the traditional structure, which had remained static and unchanged for so long.

It is important to remember that these broad-scale, long-term changes continued to transform the Dominican Republic in a fundamental way, irrespective of the fact that for more than three decades the country was brutally tyrannized by the Trujillo regime. And, despite the instability of the post-Trujillo period, the Dominican political system as a whole underwent a basic recasting and reconstruction. Political parties, representing new and diverse points of view, and the newer social sectors that had emerged during the previous era were organized or restructured. New interests began to make their weight felt in political affairs, and a wide variety of new governmental programs were initiated. At the same time, the power of the country's vested interests—the military, the elite, the Church hierarchy—remained strong. Even the more tradition-oriented sectors of the population, however, were caught up in the social and political changes that were rapidly transforming the nation. But the very modernization process—the breaking down of a traditional society and the effort to establish a new, more modern system—itself implies disruption and discontinuities. The conflicts between old and new, traditional and modern were primarily responsible for the post-Trujillo instability that occurred and that led, ultimately, to the revolution of 1965.

The Dominican Republic is thus a country in transition from underdeveloped to developed, and it has not yet permanently bridged that gap. While new and more modern institutions and practices have been introduced, the vestiges of the traditional, semifeudal order remain. While the older order is declining, it has not yet disappeared; and while a new order is rising, it has not yet been firmly established. Significantly, neither the emerging new forces nor the fading old order proved strong or able enough to govern effectively and fill the vacuum left by the collapse of the Trujillo dictatorship. In the Dominican Republic in recent years, the dynamics of change and continuity have produced an especially heady brew of violence, instability, and frequent chaos.

This conflict between the old and the new, between the modern and the traditional, is complicated by the fact that the Dominican Republic has become a point of contention in the Cold War. Clearly, the United States does not want to see a "second Cuba" established so close to home, and it intervened militarily in 1965 to put down a revolution which it thought might result in a Castro-like takeover. Most observers of Latin American affairs feel that the U.S. intervention and subsequent actions were ill advised and almost certainly self-defeating. In any case, it is certain that the interjection of Cold War issues into a country already severely divided by wide social and economic cleavages and by intensely felt ideological and political passions made the process of development and modernization in the Dominican Republic infinitely more difficult.

Chapter II

GEOGRAPHY

ESPANOLA ("LITTLE SPAIN"), as the Spaniards called it, or Hispaniola, its anglicized name, is located about midway in that long chain of Caribbean islands which stretches from Florida to Venezuela. It is separated from Cuba on the west by the Windward Passage and from Puerto Rico on the east by the Mona Passage, but both neighboring islands are almost within sight. To the north lies the Atlantic Ocean and to the south is the Caribbean Sea.

The island of Hispaniola* is shared by two countries—Haiti takes up the western third and the Dominican Republic the eastern two-thirds. In terms of population, however, the proportions are almost exactly reversed; Haiti has the larger population, with around 5 million people, while the Dominican Republic has some 3.5 million. The Dominican Republic is closing the gap, though; its population growth rate of 3.5 per cent per year is among the highest in the world.

The two countries that evolved on Hispaniola have dissimilar cultural patterns, but they share many of the same basic problems. The Dominican Republic, colonized by Spaniards, is Spanish-speaking, culturally Hispanic, racially mulatto-white, and with traditions similar to those of other Spanish American countries. Haiti, on the other hand, was colonized by the French, and its

* The island is also sometimes referred to by its pre-Columbian Indian name "Quisqueya" ("Mother of all nations"). "Hispaniola" is much more frequently used by foreigners; Dominicans use "Quisqueya" more.

10

people are French- or patois-speaking, culturally French (among the elite elements) and African, racially mulatto-Negro, and with traditions unlike those in most of Latin America. Both the Dominican Republic and Haiti, however, are characterized by widespread poverty, tempestuous political histories, the absence of democratic or constitutional traditions, and enormous social and economic problems.

Hispaniola is geographically located at a strategic point of approach to the Caribbean Sea and to the whole of Central America. It commands the major trade routes between Europe and the Isthmus of Panama and between the North American east coast and Latin America. Throughout the island's history, this strategic location has meant that Hispaniola has been subjected to successive foreign influences, raids, changes of ownership, and occupations. For the better part of five centuries, her internal politics has been shaped or determined by the international interplay of the world's great powers—particularly, in recent times, by her large North American neighbor. This point merits a brief historical digression.

The Spaniards employed Hispaniola initially as a jumping-off base for explorations and conquests of other islands and the mainland. Cortés, the conqueror of Mexico; Balboa, who crossed Darien to become the first European to look upon the Pacific from the American continent; Pizarro, who conquered present-day areas of Ecuador and Peru—all stopped first on Hispaniola. French buccaneers settled in the western end of the island in the seventeenth century, and numerous conflicts between the French and Spaniards took place. Swashbuckling pirates of several nationalities also sought to use the island as a base to prey on the Spanish fleets carrying gold and silver back from Mexico and Peru. The British invaded in 1586 and 1655 and the French again in 1689. By the Treaty of Ryswick in 1697, French claims to the western third of Hispaniola were formally and legally recognized; and this division has persisted until the present time.

In the early nineteenth century, the Haitians overthrew French rule, massacred or drove out the whites, and overran the entire island; and from 1861 to 1865 the Spanish reasserted control. As the twentieth century began, a number of European powers were threatening to send gunboats to collect unpaid debts. During the two world wars of this century, it was feared that the Germans might use the island as a submarine base. And in more recent times, the United States has seen still another outside element, Castroites and Communists, as a threat to the Dominican Republic.

As the United States itself began to emerge as a major world power in the late nineteenth century, it too began to have designs on the island. The theoretician of naval power Admiral Alfred Thayer Mahan urged that the Caribbean should become the "American Mediterranean"; and the long chain of naval and air bases that the United States still maintains throughout the Antilles attests to the continuing relevance of Mahan's analysis in contemporary strategic thinking. Sumner Welles, a former Assistant Secretary of State for Latin American Affairs and author of a well-known history of the Dominican Republic, has written:

> It may be confidently asserted that since the acquisition of the Panama Canal Zone by the United States every American Secretary of State has regarded the preservation of peace and the maintenance of the orderly procedures of government in the region of the Caribbean as a matter of deep concern to the United States. The outbreak of hostilities and the persistence of revolutionary conditions in that neighborhood have been the motives for well-founded alarm.*

U.S. interests in the Dominican Republic began long before the completion of the Panama Canal, however. Shortly after the

* *Naboth's Vineyard: The Dominican Republic, 1844–1924* (New York: Payson and Clarke, 1928), p. 925.

country achieved its independence from the Haitians in 1844, the idea of establishing a U.S. protectorate over it gained prominence, and some, both Dominicans and Americans, even talked of outright annexation. The treaty to establish a protectorate narrowly missed passage in the U.S. Senate, but the proposal of ceding to the United States rights to the Bay of Samaná (one of the two natural harbors in the country) for use as a naval base continued to be a widely discussed theme during the last third of the nineteenth century. Even today, the United States maintains a tracking station on Samaná, and Dominican nationalists are still fearful that the Bay may become a U.S. naval base.

It was in direct response to Dominican events, furthermore, that President Theodore Roosevelt in 1905 formulated his famous corollary to the Monroe Doctrine: European creditors were preparing to use force to collect unpaid Dominican debts; and, rather than permit foreign dominance of the island, the United States took over the Dominican customs receivership and began to pay off the creditors. As World War I began, the Dominican Republic's continued political instability and the added fear that a European nation might take advantage of the instability to gain control over the island and use it as a base for attacks on the United States prompted President Woodrow Wilson to authorize American troops to occupy the country.

Following the withdrawal of the Marines, in 1924, and a brief period in the Dominican Republic of more democratic rule, the Trujillo dictatorship helped protect U.S. interests in the Caribbean; and for a long time the United States supported or was benevolently neutral toward his oppressive regime, largely because he was able to maintain order and stability and because he proved to be staunchly pro-American. Later, after Trujillo's assassination, the United States poured in enormous amounts of economic and other assistance in an effort to promote a more democratic system and convert the country into a "Showcase for the Alliance for Progress," as an alternative to Castroism. If

Cuba were "only 90 miles from home," moreover, the Dominican Republic was not much farther away; and, during this period, the United States also steadfastly sought to prevent another Castroite-Communist regime from coming to power in this Caribbean nation. It was primarily for that reason that the United States again sent troops to put down the revolution of 1965.

The United States has thus for roughly 100 years maintained a vital military-political-strategic interest in this area, which was frequently referred to as "our backyard," or "mare nostrum." The Caribbean region, on the "soft underbelly" of the United States, lies in what it considers its special realm of influence; and the domestic and international politics of the countries in this area, especially since the Spanish-American War, have frequently been in large measure determined by their relations with the United States.

The strategic geographical location of Hispaniola, furthermore, has been of crucial importance to the world's powers for centuries. The constant interference in Dominican affairs by outside forces has meant that the country could not develop freely and independently on its own but has instead been subjected to severe buffeting in international crosswinds. Its key location has historically given the Dominican Republic an international significance that far exceeds what its size and resources might lead one to believe.

In size, then, the Dominican Republic is small. Its total area of approximately 19,000 square miles makes it slightly larger than Denmark or Switzerland and comparable in size to Costa Rica or the states of Vermont and New Hampshire combined. Among the Antillean islands, its area is second only to that of Cuba.

It is shaped, as many commentators have pointed out, like an isosceles triangle lying on its side. The base of the triangle is formed by the 193-mile border with Haiti, while the two sides are formed by the Atlantic Ocean and the Caribbean Sea. The tip of the triangle points east toward Puerto Rico.

The land forms in the Dominican Republic are the most complex in the Caribbean chain. Four principal mountain ranges, running parallel from southeast to northwest, cross the country. The southernmost is the Baoruco Range, the eastern extension of the chain that forms Haiti's southern peninsula. The Sierra de Neiba runs parallel to the Baoruco and slightly north of it. Stretching across the middle of the island is the giant Cordillera Central, containing Pico Duarte (formerly Pico Trujillo, which the late dictator caused to be named after himself), the highest mountain (10,300 ft.) in the West Indies. The Cordillera breaks up into several smaller ranges, some running toward the Caribbean and one, the Cordillera Oriental, stretching all the way to the eastern tip of the Dominican Republic. The northernmost range is the Cordillera Septentrional, which parallels the Atlantic coast and ends, in the Samaná Peninsula, in a series of rugged hills.

Throughout the country's history, these high mountains served to accentuate Dominican regionalism and to prevent the emergence of a modern, integrated nation-state. Transportation and communications over the mountains were difficult and hence limited; a trip from one major town to another was undertaken infrequently, and most Dominicans stayed within their own locale. As late as the 1920's, the road between the two major cities, Santo Domingo and Santiago, was little more than a muddy path, and radio and telephone communications were practically nonexistent.

Political loyalty often went primarily to one's region, rather than to the national government, which was too distant or inaccessible. Rival "first families," who usually owned much of the land in their particular regions, also controlled social life and politics. Regional *caudillos* would band together to overthrow the national government until they were likewise overthrown.

Most Dominicans, however, were unaffected by what occurred at the national level; their life revolved around local society or the local *patrón*, who in a paternalistic way looked after their needs. Little sense of national identity or loyalty developed.

During the long Trujillo era, 1930–61, which in many ways signified a turning point in Dominican history, localism and regionalism were effectively broken down. Trujillo demanded absolute loyalty to the nation (himself) before loyalty to any local leader, and he manipulated nationalistic sentiments to build up a feeling of "Dominicanism." He completed the destruction of the power of the regional *caudillos* and sought to curtail the power of the country's elite families. By the time Trujillo was assassinated, a strong sense of nationalism had developed, and the power of the central state was clearly far superior to that of the provinces.

Transportation and communications among the several regions also improved greatly during the Trujillo era. Other than the private lines used for hauling cane on the larger sugar plantations, there is only a single commercial railroad—connecting the rich farm lands of the northern Cibao Valley with the port of Sánchez on Samaná Bay—and even this single line has fallen into disuse. But the primary and secondary road system developed by Trujillo is excellent. Three major highways fan out to the east, west, and north from the capital, Santo Domingo, on the southern coast, and they connect all the major towns. Paved secondary roads feed into these three major highways, creating an effective web over most of the country.

Along the Haitian border, in a hilly area where few people live, and across the rugged Cordillera Central, there are still very few roads. And because the lack of farm-to-market roads is so widespread, many perishable agricultural products cannot be sold in a large market. (Fruits and vegetables that have to travel part of the distance to market by mule or burro spoil before they get there.) Finally, some of the supposedly public highways built during the Trujillo era led only to the dictator's private estates. (One expensive suspension bridge, built by the Generalissimo, is now used only as a footbridge because it empties into a vacant field.) Despite these limitations, transportation in the Dominican Republic is better than in almost all other Central American nations; the most remote areas of the country are seldom more than five hours by car from the capital.

The communications media also improved greatly during Trujillo's regime. The number of radios and radio stations multiplied, and two television stations were established. Newspaper circulation also increased. Improved public transportation in the form of buses and public cars (*públicos*) in turn contributed to the more rapid expansion of the famed Dominican rumor network (Radio Bemba). Though during Trujillo's dictatorship the expanding communications media were employed to further the cult of the Generalissimo, the framework for a modern communications system was established.

Because its land forms are the most complex in the Antilles, the Dominican Republic has a wide variety of climatic patterns. It is a tropical country, but the island's temperatures are moderated somewhat by high elevations, trade winds, and the surrounding water. In lowland areas, such as the capital city, it is hot all year around; the average annual temperature is about 78° F., and it rarely gets below 70° F. Winter temperatures in the mountains near Constanza, by way of contrast, may drop below freezing.

Rainfall is also widely varied. Where the trade winds sweep in from the ocean, such as at Samaná, more than 100 inches of rain may fall each year. On the opposite side of the country, such as at Barahona and Montecristi (the base points of our tipped isosceles triangle), it is desert-dry. Natural vegetation likewise varies from the tropical rainforests of the valleys, to the savannas of the mesas, to the pine forests of the Cordillera Central, to the cactus of the southwest.

High mountains, the variety of climatic patterns, and the differing natural vegetation contributed to and reinforced regional differences in the country. The east, with its broad, gently sloping savannas, is primarily sugar-cane and secondarily cattle-raising country. These savannas, largely devoid of trees but with vast grazing lands and acre after acre of gently swaying cane, stretch from the capital city to the easternmost tip of the island, and from the Caribbean Coast to the foothills of the Cordillera Oriental just below Samaná Bay. The U.S.–owned South Puerto Rico Sugar Company holds much of the land in this area. Two ports on the southern coast, La Romana and San Pedro de Macorís, are the largest cities in the east.

In the center of the island, the mountains dominate. Some population centers may be found in the rich valleys between the ranges, but in the Cordillera Central few people are able to eke out a living. The scarcity of topsoil, washed away down the deforested mountains, results in a near-empty land that stretches all the way to the Haitian border. A few subsistence peasants scratch out a meager existence in the mountain region, but much of the land is deserted and unexplored. (While the mountains provide good cover, the fact that few peasants live in this area makes it extremely difficult to launch a successful guerrilla movement in the Dominican Republic. The guerrillas who took to the hills in 1963 were unable to obtain sufficient food or popular support and their movement was quickly crushed.)

The northern part of the country contains the agricultural heartland—the Cibao Valley and the Vega Real (Royal Valley). The Vega Real is a flat savanna with hip-high grasses that stretches eastward from the peak at Santo Cerro near La Vega as far as the eye can see. Tobacco, cacao, some rice, and cattle are raised in this rich area. There are few trees, and gently flowing streams run through the plains, emptying into the Yuma

River (which, in turn, empties into Samaná Bay). The Vega Real is proudly considered by Dominicans to be one of the special glories of their land.

The Cibao, nestled between the Cordillera Central and the Cordillera Septentrional, dominates the Dominican Republic's north. It is 140 miles long and nine to twenty-eight miles wide, with fertile soil, particularly the coal-black loam variety that occurs between Moca and San Francisco de Macorís. The Cibao has historically been the center of most of the country's landed elite families. Its central city, Santiago de los Caballeros, is still much more traditional than the capital, and its inhabitants take pride in the fact that the girls are friendlier, prettier, and more personable and the people more courteous. Horse-drawn carriages still carry couples around the central squares and to Saturday night dances. Even today, Santiago—and the surrounding Cibao—contains many of the most prominent and most well-to-do, as well as some of the best-educated and most able, Dominican families.

Sugar is also produced on the narrow Atlantic coastal strip that lies over the Cordillera Septentrional from the Cibao. At the Cibao Valley's western extremity is the hot and dry area where the United Fruit Company in times past grew bananas; at the eastern end is located Samaná Peninsula.

In the south, midway along the Caribbean coast, lies the capital city of Santo Domingo, which in recent decades has grown into a big, busy, sprawling metropolis. The downtown sector— where the "Constitutionalists" were centered during the 1965 revolution—is old and traditional, some of the buildings dating back to Columbus; the outlying areas are modern. Some of the country's worst slums—into which the police will not even venture—are also to be found here. Santo Domingo is not only the seat of government but also the social and economic center of the country.

Westward from Santo Domingo along the narrow southern

coast, a single road winding through Baní and Azua leads into the southwest, the most poverty-ridden and most Haiti-like section of the country. Much of it is desert where very poor, starving people struggle against disease, lack of water, poor land, and almost no educational facilities. A spur off the Azua–Barahona road leads between the Baoruco Range and the Sierra de Neiba to the salt-water Lake Enriquillo, which at 150 feet below sea level is the lowest point in the West Indies. Another spur goes up a more prosperous valley between the Sierra de Neiba and the Cordillera Central to San Juan de la Maguana. Some sugar is raised around Barahona, and the Alcoa company mines bauxite near Cabo Rojo, but the southwest is still the most barren of the Dominican regions.

Most Dominicans—70 per cent—live in rural areas, while the remaining 30 per cent live in towns of 1,000 or more. These rural-urban percentages reflect the fact that the country is still basically agricultural rather than industrial. Fully one-third of all those considered urban dwellers live in Santo Domingo, whose population is close to 350,000. The second largest city, Santiago, has a population of around 100,000.

Other than Santo Domingo and Santiago, there are no metropolitan centers in the country. But there are many towns whose population ranges from 15,000 to 35,000. These include Azua, Baní, Barahona, San Juan de la Maguana, La Romana, San Pedro de Macorís, Montecristi, Puerto Plata, Moca, La Vega, and San Francisco de Macorís. In recent years many peasants in search of jobs, better living standards, and more social amenities have migrated from the countryside to these urban areas, especially Santo Domingo, with the result that the populations of the cities have multiplied, their slums have mushroomed, and an entirely new set of social, economic, and political problems has been created.

While Santo Domingo is the largest city in the country, the nucleus of population is still in the rich Cibao area. Together with the adjoining northern coast, this region contains more than half the total population of the country. Another third live along the southern coastal plain from San Cristóbal to La Romana, a strip that includes the metropolitan area of greater Santo Domingo. Most of the rest are scattered along the southwest coast, in the extreme northwest and northeast, and in the geographical center. The country is not notably overpopulated; its over-all density of population is 140 per square mile, which is low for the islands of the West Indies but high in comparison with the mainland of Latin America.

The Dominican Republic has a wide variety of mostly untapped mineral resources. Though a few gold nuggets may still be found, gold mining on the island was never a very prosperous enterprise and ceased almost entirely after the discovery of far richer deposits in Mexico and Peru in the early sixteenth century. However, some oil is pumped from the ground at Azua; some iron is mined at Hatillo Maimon, bauxite in the southwest, marble at Samaná; and small amounts of nickel, gold, gypsum, sulphur, and copper may be found in scattered places. Salt is taken from the sea at Azua, Baní, and Montecristi, and the ten-mile-long mountain of rock salt (the world's largest) at Neiba provides an almost inexhaustible supply. Former President Juan Bosch kept small bottles containing samples of these minerals in his home and planned to begin a program to find and exploit the untapped wealth of the country, but he was overthrown before the project could be initiated.

The outstanding resource of the Dominican Republic, however, is an abundance of good agricultural land. Between the mountain ranges lie some of the most fertile valleys to be found in the Americas. Chief of these are the Vega Real, the Cibao, and the savannas of the east; but throughout the island are many smaller, but no less fertile, areas of rich land. Much of this land is unexploited—estimates indicate that only about 23 per cent of the country's total area is being cultivated or used for pasture.

What emerges from this consideration of the Dominican Republic's geography is a picture of a country that, because of its strategic location, has often been subject to interference by larger powers; and that, because it is geographically divided into separate and widely differing regions, did not until recently emerge as a unified nation with a sense of national identity. It is a diverse country with a variety of land forms, vegetation, and climatic patterns, which have had an enormous influence on the life styles of the peoples in the various regions. Finally, it is a potentially wealthy country, particularly agriculturally, and one in which some of the basic prerequisites for the emergence of a more integrated nation—such as communications and transportation networks—have been established. How these resources have been developed and employed will be our concern in the following chapters.

Chapter III

THE PATTERN OF HISTORICAL DEVELOPMENT

WHILE IN MANY respects nature has been bountiful to the island of Hispaniola, history has been considerably less kind. This was well stated by the distinguished American writer Washington Irving, who wrote in 1828 that this was "one of the most beautiful islands in the world and doomed to be one of the most unfortunate."

Hispaniola has had many firsts. The island was one of the first to be discovered by Columbus on his initial voyage. Columbus admired the beauty of Hispaniola, believed that there was more wealth for the taking there than on the other islands he visited, and determined that it should be settled. The first colony in the New World was hence established on the north coast, but its settlers were soon slain by the indigenous Indians. A second colony was then established, but reports of more gold farther south led to the abandonment of the northern outpost and the founding of Santo Domingo de Guzmán on the banks of the Ozama River, destined to become the first permanent European city in the Western Hemisphere.

Spain's earliest experiments in colonial government were conducted here. In fact, many of the colonial institutions tried out on Hispaniola Spain later used to rule its extensive colonial empire in the Americas. In Santo Domingo, the first viceregal court and the first *audiencia* (a judicial, advisory, and legislative body) were established. The oldest cathedral, the oldest monastery, the oldest university, and the oldest hospital in the New World were founded on the island. Hispaniola was also the scene of Latin America's first revolution.

From the beginning, a rigid, hierarchical social class system was established. Patterning the colony on the model of the Spanish court and society, Columbus' brother Bartolomé and son Diego established themselves and a few others as the nobility; artisans, craftsmen, and soldiers formed the small middle class; and the native Indians became servants and slaves. Class and caste lines were tightly drawn, and few moved from one socio-economic level to another.

This structure persisted into the modern era with few basic changes. The indigenous population soon died off and was replaced by slaves imported from Africa. In the nineteenth century, furthermore, during the Haitian occupations, the old elite was either killed or fled the country, and it was not until later in the century that a new oligarchy began to emerge. But the system of rigid class-caste stratification remained constant. Juan Bosch has persuasively argued that this system provided the psychological motivation for the rise to power of the dictator Trujillo, who was born of a middle-class family and aspired above all to be a part of the elite. The tightly drawn hierarchical structure has also been used to explain the overthrow of Bosch's own government, which faced the concerted opposition of the country's powerful established interests when it attempted to govern for and in the name of the lower classes.

During the first half-century of Spanish rule, Hispaniola flourished, for it served as an administrative center and as a base for the expeditions of the conquistadors to neighboring lands. But the more lucrative conquests of Mexico and Peru soon turned it into a poor way-station. In search of gold and glory, the most ambitious and enterprising Europeans emigrated to the more attractive mainland. During the same period the

Indians were decimated, not so much by the force of the Spanish conquerors' arms as by the diseases the Spaniards carried with them from Europe for which the native Quisqueyans had no immunity. (Santo Domingo provided Hans Zinnser with a major example to prove the thesis of his book *Rats, Lice, and History*, that the diseases carried by rats and lice have decided more battles throughout history than has the force of arms.)

By 1550, Hispaniola had been almost abandoned. There was relatively little silver or gold to be found, and hence the colony was of little value to the Spanish Crown. For the better part of three centuries of colonial rule, it remained a neglected, poverty-ridden corner of the vast Spanish empire. On the other end of the island, by way of contrast, French Saint-Domingue, based on a slave plantation system, meanwhile grew to become the world's richest colonial possession.

During the eighteenth century, the Spanish colony experienced a resurgence of prosperity. Sugar and coffee plantations and cattle ranches stimulated foreign trade and commerce, and the landowners and merchants prospered. More Negro slaves were brought in, and a new wave of Spaniards immigrated from the Canary Islands to strengthen the Crown's hold. Despite some improvements, however, Hispaniola still remained poor in comparison with Spain's other colonies. By 1789, its population was still only 125,000 (of which about 15,000 were slaves), while that of the far more prosperous French colony numbered half a million. There were still few roads and little internal trade, and in the rural areas even the wealthy went barefoot.

Because of its poverty and neglect, curiously, Hispaniola experienced much of the worst of the Spanish colonial heritage. The slave society established in the sixteenth century evolved into a feudal order in the eighteenth and nineteenth centuries. Each class or sector—at least theoretically—had its own rights and privileges as well as its own duties and responsibilities. In fact, however, a very few people monopolized almost all the wealth and power while the vast mass of the population, forced to labor for the few, lived in abysmal poverty. A middle class was virtually nonexistent.

The governmental structure was one of a hierarchy of despots —from king, to captain general, to local *hacendado* (landowner) —all of whom exercised absolute power within their respective jurisdictions. No tradition of self-government, democracy, or popular participation in local affairs developed.

The Roman Catholic Church frequently served as an arm of the government and was often characterized by an authoritarianism that paralleled the state's. Though few priests came to such an abandoned and poor colony after the initial flurry of discovery, Hispaniola was "Christianized" right from the beginning, and its later immigrants, mostly African slaves, were persuaded or forced to accept the faith. Today, according to the official figures, the country is 98 per cent Roman Catholic. In this setting, freedom of religion was not possible, and church and state were mutually supporting institutions.

The economy was one of exploitation. What there was of natural wealth was drained off for the enrichment of Spain rather than being reinvested in the local economy. Even at present, as we shall see, the country's economy is geared for production for the world market rather than for local consumption and self-sufficiency.

Throughout its colonial history, indeed, Hispaniola provides a particularly vivid illustration of the way in which an exploitative, authoritarian, colonial government can be an instrument of ruin. The native population had been decimated and the wealth of the island plundered. Perhaps nowhere in the Americas was there a history of greater continuous spoliation and destruction of human life and material resources. It is thus easy to see why, when Spain's colonial control dissolved in the early nineteenth century, the country was left with practically no native tradition. Hispaniola was by-passed by all the great and far-reaching revolutions of the modern world—the Protestant Reformation, the scientific revolution, the industrial revolution, and the growth of democratic and representative rule; its intellectual, religious, economic, and political traditions and institutions remained rooted not in the modern but in the medieval era. The colonial era bequeathed a legacy that the Dominican Republic has not yet overcome.

After three centuries of colonial rule, Spain, defeated in Europe, ceded its eastern two-thirds of the island to France in 1795. Due to the more pressing needs of the same European wars, however, France was not able effectively to control the island either. And, led by former slaves Toussaint L'Ouverture and Jean-Jacques Dessalines, the French colony rose up in a bloody revolt which resulted not only in independence from Napoleonic rule but also in the death or flight of the white European elite and the destruction of their plantations. In 1805, Dessalines, another former slave, Henri Christophe (after whom Eugene O'Neill apparently patterned his play *Emperor Jones*), and the black armies under their command invaded the Spanish-speaking end of the island, instilling terror in the white ruling class there. With the aid of the English fleet, which hoped to capture this rich colonial prize, the Haitians were driven out; and in 1809, at a time when the other Latin American areas were beginning to seek independence from the mother country, the colony was reunited with Spain.

The independence of Spanish Haiti, as it was then called, was proclaimed in 1821 by José Nuñez de Cáceres. This time, independence lasted nine weeks. In the face of the continuing threat of a Haitian invasion, envoys were sent to Simón Bolívar, the great Liberator, seeking the help of Gran Colombia. But before the needed assistance could be secured, Haitian columns under the mulatto general Jean Pierre Boyer again overran the newly independent nation and declared the union of the island.

The Haitian occupation, 1822–44, was cruel and barbarous.

Haitians held the highest offices; closed the university; severed the Church's ties with Rome; disrupted the economy, which had begun to prosper in the previous century; forced out the traditional ruling class; and came near to exterminating all the whites. Sumner Welles' two-volume history concludes that the basic cause of the anarchy, unrest, chaos, and dictatorship that was to characterize Dominican independent history was the near obliteration of European civilization during the twenty-two-year Haitian occupation.

The Dominican Republic's long struggle for independence—from France, from Haiti, from Spain, and then from Haiti again—lasted for half a century; but when independence finally came, Dominicans were ill prepared for it. Juan Pablo Duarte, the country's great independence leader and national hero, organized a secret society, La Trinitaria, which led the struggle; and finally in 1844 the Haitians were driven out. But Duarte and the other heroes of independence, Ramón Mella and Francisco del Rosario Sánchez, were soon exiled, and the independent nation's future was left in other, less noble hands.

From 1844 until 1899, three dictators—Pedro Santana, Buenaventura Báez, and Ulises Heureaux—dominated Dominican history. The noted historian of Latin America Hubert Herring calls all three "brazen opportunists, ready to betray their country for their own ends" and states that "nowhere else has *personalismo*—the rule of the boss—been more persistent than in this weak nation."* While the *form* of government was always democratic and representative, with a three-part division of powers, as in the United States Constitution, Dominican political realities greatly diverged from the legal and constitutional forms.

Santana and Báez emerged as the two most prominent leaders in the newly independent republic. For many years, they alter-

* *A History of Latin America* (New York: Alfred A. Knopf, 1957), pp. 425–26.

nated in power and in the process almost destroyed the infant country. The exercise of sheer power, based on the personal allegiance of armed camp followers, was the method of articulating political views; revolutions and civil war were the means for effecting political change. In this atmosphere, no tradition of constitutionalism or of representative democracy could be established.

Santana became convinced that the country could not defend itself against Haiti's assaults, which had been nearly continuous even after 1844; and in 1861, the Dominican Republic was again placed under the control of Spain, Santana being named governor-general. Spanish rule proved inept and unprofitable, however, and in 1865, Isabella II, with a timely push from Dominican forces, withdrew her troops.

The idea of a protectorate nevertheless remained, and Báez approached the United States with a plan. The questionable—and highly colorful—involvement of an American land-speculating company led by the beautiful and adventurous Jane Cazneau, who used her considerable talents and feminine wiles to lobby in favor of the establishment of a protectorate, was uncovered, however; and the U.S. Senate failed to ratify the treaty.

During the 1870's, the country passed through a period of more instability. Báez returned to the presidency for the fifth time but was later driven into exile. The country's first, but short-lived, democratic government under Ulises Espaillat came to power, but the tenure of this idealistic president did not last long either. The chaos culminated in the emergence of a new strong man, Ulises Heureaux, in 1882.

"Lilís" Heureaux's rule, described by Herring as "perhaps the most pitiless tyranny in the history of Latin America," lasted for the next seventeen years. Another historian of Dominican affairs, Selden Rodman, has written, "Only by looking ahead to the equally ruthless and 'successful' career of Rafael Leonidas

Trujillo Molina in our time can any accurate comparisons be found for the method and madness of Ulises Heureaux."* He bought up many of his rivals and subjected most of the rest to vilification, exile, or murder; employed an army of spies (including his former mistresses); sent assassins abroad; and enriched himself, his friends, and his relatives at the expense of the nation. Rodman concludes:

> Only in respect to the techniques of the modern totalitarian state, still to be invented by Hitler and Stalin—the single party, the mass rallies, the propaganda mills, the rewriting of history, the indoctrination of children, the racial persecution, the military juggernaut —did Ulises Heureaux yield anything in refinements of despotism to his infamous successor.

Following Heureaux's assassination in 1899, the country returned to the chaos that had gone before. Four revolutions took place and five presidents gained office in six years. For a brief period, under the able leadership of Ramón Cáceres, the Dominican Republic seemed to be recovering, but civil war began again after he was assassinated. In a desperate attempt to stop the constant bickering among rival first family groups and to avert more of the continuous upheaval and instability, the Archbishop of Santo Domingo, Adolfo Nouel, was elevated to the presidency. But even he was forced to resign, and disorder broke out once more.

In the meantime, the policies of Báez, Heureaux, and their successors, of raising revenues by simply printing more money and by floating ruinous foreign loans, had brought the country to the verge of bankruptcy. Rather than permitting the European nations to send battleships to collect these unpaid debts—as they were threatening to do—the United States took over the administration of the customs house, the major source of gov-

* *Quisqueya: A History of the Dominican Republic* (Seattle: University of Washington Press, 1964), p. 92.

ernment revenues, and began to pay back the foreign loans. But this did not prevent the political situation from degenerating still further into anarchy. In 1916, fearing that the continuing chaos might lead to the domination of the strategically located island by a hostile foreign power, urged on by self-serving diplomatic representatives, and no doubt motivated by idealistic zeal to spread the "benefits of democracy," President Wilson authorized U.S. military forces to occupy the country.

During the United States occupation, 1916–24, the Dominican Congress was suspended, the Supreme Court stripped of its authority, and the U.S. military governor granted power to rule by decree. The occupation forces improved the sanitation, communications, and educational facilities and engaged in other constructive projects, but the U.S. Marines assumed arbitrary power and at times abused their authority. Patriotic Dominicans of all shades of opinion disapproved of the occupation, and some engaged in a guerrilla campaign against the U.S. forces.

The Marine occupation had a number of long-range effects, too. The construction of roads helped to break down localism and regionalism. Centralization resulted from an assertion of control over the municipalities and from divesting the provincial governors of their military authority. Perhaps the major immediate effect was the creation of a modern unified constabulary, for it was through the constabulary that the future dictator, Trujillo, was to rise to power. Dominican nationalists like Noel Henríquez called him "the bastard son of the occupation forces,"* and it is primarily for this reason that the United States is still often held accountable by Dominicans for the corruption and terrorism of the entire Trujillo era.

A new constitution was promulgated in 1924, and Horacio Vásquez was elected president. For the first time in nearly two decades, a combination of relative freedom and order existed.

* *La verdad sobre Trujillo* (Havana: Imp. Económica en General, 1959), pp. 92–93.

But Vásquez alienated friends and enemies alike by swelling the government with his relatives and by extending his term of office from four to six years. In 1929, the president became seriously ill, and while he was in the United States receiving medical treatment, conspiracies against his government were incubated. Moreover, the world depression critically hurt the all-important Dominican sugar industry, with the result that the economy was near collapse.

The following year, 1930, a revolution led by Rafael Estrella Ureña was launched from Santiago. The National Army, by this time under the firm control of Trujillo, failed to come to the aid of the tottering government, which quickly fell. That same year, Trujillo himself gained the presidency, and his lengthy reign began.

The history of the pre-Trujillo Dominican Republic was thus characterized by successive dictatorships and revolutions, anarchy and civil wars, foreign interventions that drained its meager wealth, and apparently insoluble economic and social problems. It had remained essentially a traditional, pre-industrial, agrarian, and semifeudal society. Trujillo's own remark is revealing:

> In 1930 our situation was still at its starting point. After eighty-six years of bloody warfare, social unrest, poverty and want, we had failed to solve any of our problems. There were still no schools, no hospitals, no employment, no boundary, no roads, no banks, no agriculture, no industry (except the sugar latifundium), no public buildings, no social security, no electric power, no university, no irrigation system, no bridges, no money, no appreciable direction.*

The Dominican pattern had been one of recurrent periods of utter chaos and of absolute despotism; its leadership had correspondingly seemed to alternate between ineffectual idealists such

* *The Evolution of Democracy in Santo Domingo* (Ciudad Trujillo: Official Publication of the Dominican Government, 1950), p. 12.

as Duarte and Espaillat, and despicable dictators like Santana, Báez, and Heureaux. It was a poor and underdeveloped country, and the divisions between groups, classes, and individuals were deep and often bitter. No tradition of democratic and representative government had been established. During its independent history, between 1844 and 1930, the country had fifty presidents (one every 1.7 years) and thirty revolutions (one every 2.9 years). With the exception of Venezuela, the Dominican Republic had had more constitutions (twenty-two) than any other country in the world. This spectacle caused Miguel Angel Monclús, in his study of Dominican caudilloism, to cry out, "Where will it stop?"* It stopped—at least temporarily—in 1930 with the coming to power of Trujillo.

* *El Caudillismo en la República Dominicana* (Ciudad Trujillo: Imp. Dominicana, 1948), p. 157.

Chapter IV

THE TRUJILLO REGIME

THE TRUJILLO REGIME was probably the strongest and most absolute dictatorship ever established in Latin America, and perhaps also the most personal dictatorship on either side of the Iron Curtain. Trujillo did not share power with anyone but maintained all authority in his own hands. His regime was neither leftist nor rightist, neither Nazi nor Fascist, for Trujillo's system represented essentially the story of a single individual and his personal power. Under his control, the Dominican Republic became—at least until the emergence of a Communist Cuba under Fidel Castro—the most nearly totalitarian regime in the history of the hemisphere.

Rafael Leonidas Trujillo Molina was born on October 24, 1891, in San Cristóbal, a poverty-stricken agricultural village on the Dominican Republic's south coast. His father was a small-time businessman and worked as a postal clerk, and young Rafael was the fourth of eleven children. Like their community, the Trujillo family was poor (although "middle class," by San Cristóbal standards), and to supplement his insufficient income Trujillo's father was reputed to have occasionally rustled cattle.

Little is known of Trujillo's early years. Official accounts say that he was taught to read by his maternal grandmother, and there is a record of his having attended grammar school. It is more likely, however, that Trujillo, like other youths of his time and circumstances, received most of his early education in the streets of San Cristóbal. He worked for a time as a telegraph operator and was the head of a private police force on one of the large sugar plantations. Here, his enemies have subsequently claimed, he learned the cruel and oppressive methods which he later applied to others. Some critics of his regime report that he was a hoodlum, cattle rustler, forger, torturer, informer, and murderer and that he had been convicted on two occasions and escaped punishment for other offenses only by fleeing. The validity of these charges cannot be ascertained with certainty since a fire in the Dominican Supreme Court building in 1927 destroyed the criminal records. For the official biographers of Trujillo, however, who later wrote laudatory accounts of his early years, it is likely that this was a providential fire.

Trujillo was twenty-four when the U.S. Marines occupied the country in 1916. An uncle introduced him to some officers of the occupation forces, and he soon joined the Dominican national constabulary created by the United States. In 1919, he received a commission, and thereafter his rise was meteoric. He was promoted to captain in 1922 and became a major in 1924. (It is reported that Trujillo achieved his promotion by arranging for the assassination of another major by a jealous husband.) He was also appointed military administrator of the northern section of the country. By distinguishing himself as a hard and efficient worker, Trujillo attracted the favorable attention of President Vásquez. In 1926, he was advanced to lieutenant colonel, and in 1928 he was promoted to chief-of-staff of what was then called the National Army.

Through adroit maneuvering and handling of promotions and appointments, Trujillo turned the Army into his personal instrument and thus became the most powerful man in the country. When, in 1930, Rafael Estrella Ureña led his revolution against the Vásquez government, Trujillo's troops remained in their barracks. After Vásquez had resigned, Trujillo collected the arms of Estrella Ureña's rebel forces. He then secured the nomination of the political parties that had opposed the President, forced the withdrawal of all other candidates through terror and persecution, and was "elected" president of the country. (In some areas, Trujillo received more votes than there were registered voters.) From 1930 until his assassination on May 30, 1961, Trujillo ruled the Dominican Republic with an iron fist.

Trujillo looked like and had the manner of a leader. He was well built and, at 5' 9", taller than most of his fellow Dominicans. He was healthy, vigorous, *macho* (very much a man), and sometimes haughty and aloof. In his dress uniforms, he looked very much like the imposing dictator that he was.

Trujillo had many of the stylistic qualities required of a Latin American political leader. He was flamboyant and seemed to have a natural flair for the dramatic. The Dominican Republic was his stage, and he was a naturally talented but also carefully self-trained and cultivated actor. He thought of himself—and was thought of by his subjects—as a national *patrón*, a great teacher and father who must lead his humble people. He could thus be kind and generous to friends and relatives and ruthlessly cruel to opponents and enemies.

He was not a good public speaker. His high-pitched voice seemed ludicrous for a political leader. He was also a megalomaniac who demanded and received constant adulation. He was intensely ambitious and thought it a shame that so large a talent as his should be confined to so small a country. He was driven by a desire for power and personal aggrandizement. Of middle-class parentage in a poor and often oppressed country, Trujillo desired a more important rank—both for himself and for his nation.

The key to Trujillo's long personal grip on the Dominican Republic was perhaps that he worked harder and longer than any of his rivals or subordinates. In addition to being an indefatigable worker, Trujillo was also an excellent organizer and administrator. Though without much formal education, he was astute, intelligent, and a master politician of the Machiavellian sort. Furthermore, he seems to have known his country, its people, and its history better than any other leader before or after him.

The armed forces were the first and most important instrument of Trujillo's control over the Dominican Republic. It had been through the national constabulary that he had risen to prominence, with Army backing that he had seized the presidency, and by the might of the armed forces that he remained in power. The dictator never allowed the reins of control over the military to slip from his hands, and he used this juggernaut not so much for purposes of national defense as to impose an all-pervasive terror upon the domestic population.

Prior to 1916, the country's armed forces had been weak and divided. Their recruits were untrained, their weapons obsolete, their ranks disorganized and mutinous, and their officers too numerous. The U.S. Marines created the first centralized, efficient, and professionalized Dominican armed force, and Trujillo carried the work of the Marines forward. He gave it modern weapons and techniques and vastly increased its size until the Dominican military was one of the largest and strongest in the Caribbean area.

Realizing that the armed forces were not only the final source of his power but also the greatest potential threat to his continued rule, Trujillo maintained an absolute personal control over them. He assigned the highest ranks to his relatives. Officers were frequently moved up and down the military hierarchy and from service to service to ensure that they were not in one command long enough to build up a personal following that might pose a challenge to the regime. The entire military was pampered and given special rights, and its officers were permitted to supplement their incomes by illegal business activities and "protection" rackets. In this way, Trujillo kept the continued loyalty of the armed forces and used them to bolster his regime.

The mere presence of the armed forces, loyal to and under the control of Trujillo, was sufficient to discourage opposition. Nevertheless, the dictator used the military apparatus to secure his terroristic control. Secret police and espionage agencies (which also checked each other) rendered any deviation from the official line dangerous. By means such as those previously developed in Stalin's Russia and Hitler's Germany, Trujillo imposed, particularly in the years after World War II, a vigilant and unremitting surveillance over every aspect of Dominican life.

Throughout the country, one was never far from the secret police. The police were suspected of being present at every gathering, whether in the flesh or by means of a hidden microphone. Mail and public-information media were censored. Indifference toward the regime was considered opposition; no one was allowed to remain neutral. Those who failed to conform were tortured or brainwashed until their collaboration was assured. Trujillo's regime was a classic cloak-and-dagger regime, complete with spies, informers, hidden microphones, and the mysterious missing persons or "accidents" that strained credibility. At times, Trujillo's terror reached outside the Dominican Republic to victims in Puerto Rico, New York, Havana, and elsewhere.

The second major instrument of Trujillo's regime was his control over the entire governmental and political apparatus. With the Army's help he had gained the presidency in 1930 and thereafter he controlled absolutely the institutional and political machinery of the state. At times, Trujillo was sure enough of his control over the country to step down from the presidency in favor of a puppet. But although he was out of office, he never relinquished any real power.

Trujillo ruled as a dictator, but he was careful to give the impression of governing according to the constitution. The constitution did not limit his authority, but it did provide a façade of legitimacy to his regime. For example, an elaborate bill of rights was promulgated, yet the classic freedoms existed only on paper. The constitution provided for the traditional three-part division of powers, but the courts and the Congress were not independent and usually functioned only to serve Trujillo or pay homage to him. Elections were held regularly, but Trujillo and his handpicked candidates always received 100 per cent of the vote—unless the dictator willed otherwise. (One "opposition" candidate for the presidency gave the game away by signing a petition favoring Trujillo's re-election.) Local and provincial autonomy gave way to the highly centralized machinery of the dictatorship.

As Trujillo's activities expanded, the bureaucracy also grew. Although the government workers were capable of efficiently handling routine tasks, they were in fact only messenger boys or servants of the regime. Elaborate loyalty checks were required, and loyalty and fidelity to the dictator, rather than competence, were highly rewarded. The same game of musical chairs that was played in the armed forces—that is, the constant shuffling of personnel—was also played in the bureaucracy. Trujillo demanded from all public officials a signed but undated resignation when they took office. When the congressman, bureaucrat, or Supreme Court justice had outlived his usefulness, Trujillo filled in the date.

A single official party, the Partido Dominicano (PD), functioned as the arm of the regime and rendered special services for it. The party did not have a genuine popular following; only as a sideline did it present candidates for election, and it never became an independent political organization. Rather, Trujillo used it to rubber-stamp his decisions and implement his programs. The PD, for example, dispensed charity—always in Trujillo's name. It gathered signatures on a petition asking that the name of the capital be changed from Santo Domingo to Ciudad Trujillo and rounded up gigantic crowds called "civic reviews" to yell "Viva!" when Trujillo appeared in public.

The Partido Dominicano maintained offices throughout the

country that kept in touch with local needs and served as the eyes and ears of the dictatorship. It kept elaborate intelligence files on politically active Dominicans and all foreign residents. (A school of home economics was used as a disguise to train maids to be informers.) The party was also employed as a clearing house for many of Trujillo's private business transactions, and it became one of the few profit-making political organizations in the world. Periodically, its funds were transferred to Trujillo's own pocket.

The entire governmental system was thus a parody of constitutionalism and democracy. Despite occasional appearances to the contrary, Trujillo alone exercised authority.

The third major instrument of Trujillo's control over the Dominican Republic was the near-monopoly he established over the national economy and over all socio-economic groups. The country was converted into his personal fief. The Dominican armed forces guarded his vast agricultural, industrial, and commercial holdings; the national territory was his field of operations; the government was his legal servant, the populace his labor force, producer, and consumer. In transforming the Dominican Republic into a vast private estate, Trujillo was perhaps "more Croesus than Caesar." It has been estimated that 50–60 per cent of the arable land (or some 700,000 acres) belonged to him or his family and that Trujillo-owned enterprises accounted for about 80 per cent of the volume of business in Ciudad Trujillo. The exact nature and extent of his holdings are impossible to determine, since the ruling family preferred to work through dummy corporations or register ownership under false names. Frequently, these properties were bought from or sold to the government (also controlled, of course, by the Trujillos), and it was sometimes difficult to judge where Trujillo's holdings ended and those of the government began. Dominicans used to say that, if a business lost money, it must be the government's; if it made money, it must be Trujillo's.

Thus, in an extremely poor country, with an average per capita income of around $200 per year, Trujillo accumulated an estate valued at around $800 million. As in most dictatorships, the streets were kept clean and great public works and buildings were constructed, but relatively little of Trujillo's huge income was reinvested in the Dominican Republic. Few, if any, public projects were initiated that did not materially benefit the Trujillo regime or family.

Trujillo's control over the national economy enabled him to impose an even tighter grip on the population. It has been estimated that about three-quarters of the employed population worked for Trujillo, either in the government or in his many agricultural, commercial, and industrial enterprises. Since the most efficient method of terror is hunger, and since almost every Dominican depended on Trujillo for his livelihood, his control over the population was assured. As Daniel James wrote, "It is impossible to eat, drink, smoke, or dress without in some way benefitting *el benefactor* or his family. The Dominican pays him tribute from birth to death."* Forced to produce and consume his products, the Dominican people were the ultimate guarantors of Trujillo's continued rule.

A spirit of fraud impregnated all government and business dealings. Legislation was designed to benefit Trujillo's business empire; and the tax structure, the national banking system, and customs and tariffs worked for the enrichment of the ruling family and its friends. For example, Trujillo's sugar companies had a special tax exemption; government-owned construction equipment was used to clear land and build refineries; the cane was planted on lands watered by government irrigation projects; access roads were built with government funds; soldiers and convicts formed the labor force; the armed forces stood guard

* Quoted in Juan Bosch, *Trujillo* (Caracas: Grabados Nationales, 1959), p. 164.

along the barbed-wire enclosures; and Army trucks transported the sugar to Trujillo shipyards.

There was no such thing as conflict of interest; the cruder forms of economic exploitation flourished, and private capital was made of the public domain. Trujillo received a 10 per cent cut of everything that the Dominican government or private business bought or sold. (At one time, a U.S. construction firm was permitted by the Internal Revenue Service to deduct the usual 10 per cent bribe as "an ordinary and necessary business expense.") And Trujillo frequently used his economic power to destroy his political enemies.

In addition to his near-monopoly of the national economic life, Trujillo kept all socio-economic groups in the country under his control. No societal sector or interest association was allowed to become a nucleus of power that could compete with the dictator's personal authority. One day the military or labor leaders would gather arm-in-arm with Trujillo before the cameras; the next day it would be the dentists, the rice growers, or the university student leaders.

The impoverished peasants (campesinos) were kept outside the social, economic, and political life of the nation and remained unorganized and ignored. Despite a few attempts to mobilize the peasantry along totalitarian lines, the dictatorship did not often bother with this group, since, unorganized, it posed no threat to the regime.

Also the labor movement was completely subservient. The unions were closely scrutinized and tightly controlled. Strikes were not permitted, freedom of association was restricted, and collective bargaining did not exist. Workers received almost no social security benefits, despite the cruel hoax of laws that existed only on paper, and slave labor was practiced in many Trujillo-owned enterprises. After Trujillo's assassination, an informal survey reported that about 90 per cent of the Dominican workers interviewed did not know what a trade union was.

Most thought that it was something "official" or like a social club.

The regime also subjected the emerging middle sectors—technicians, bureaucrats, professionals, businessmen—to tight control. These people were forced to joined the Partido Dominicano and were made dependent on the government for most of their business. Formerly respected groups such as the Rotarians, the Lawyers Association, the Masons, and the Odd Fellows were soon turned into Trujillo fronts. Though some middle-class individuals managed to remain aloof from the dictatorship, they could not organize themselves independently and were powerless to oppose it.

Even the traditional Dominican oligarchy was subjected to Trujillo's rule. Ever since Trujillo had been blackballed by one of the elite social clubs, he had demonstrated bitterness toward the oligarchy. He destroyed the centers of its social and political power and later gained control over much of its wealth. Trujillo then shuffled a few branches on his family tree and claimed to be the greatest aristocrat of them all: a direct descendant of a Spanish grandee and of a member of the Napoleonic court.

In place of the old elite, Trujillo created a "new-rich" group that was loyal to and dependent on him. Members of this new elite built ostentatious homes, had an overabundance of servants, but failed to develop much taste or social grace. However, they did provide some window dressing to his regime.

Trujillo had a political philosophy which had certain important uses, but it was neither subtle nor profound nor a full-fledged ideology of the Communist or Fascist type. His philosophy centered around ideas of peace, order, and stability; nationalism; the deification of the leader as the personification of the nation; material progress; the strong, organic, and corporate state. This ideology was not original, and the regime made no more than a half-hearted attempt to indoctrinate or brainwash the population in the official belief system. But Trujillo's philosophy did provide a rationale for his dictatorial rule. It also functioned as a rallying point for Dominican patriotism and national aspirations and helped to promote a favorable (albeit false) picture of his government abroad.

While Trujillo's political philosophy was not a full-fledged totalitarian ideology, it took on added importance when reinforced by his control over education, intellectual life, and communications, by his extensive use of public relations to project a better image, and by his reciprocal supportive arrangement with the Church.

Newspapers, radio, television, and all other means of communication had to be fully in accord with the official line emanating from the National Palace. No criticism of Trujillo was permitted. Headlines, editorials, and news stories were slanted. Reporters were told when and how to write a story; they could not independently check the facts supplied. Writers vied to praise Trujillo in an original manner, prompting a critic of the regime to remark that the only difficulty for Dominican newspapermen was to coin a new adjective. In the controlled press, the dictator used the letters-to-the-editor column to denounce "anonymously" those who had displeased Trujillo. The propaganda transmitted over radio and television was similar to that in the newspapers.

The national educational system and intellectual life were also carefully controlled. The official cult of Trujillo was the most important subject taught in the schools. The basic primer, supposedly written by Trujillo himself, glorified his virtues and lauded his rule. This kind of indoctrination was continued in the high schools and at the university level: Lectures had to be in accord with the official line; spies were planted in the classrooms; and the students were not allowed to organize or to engage in political activities. Intellectual activity was further stifled by dogmatism and the absence of creative freedom and tolerance.

During his lifetime, Trujillo was compared with lightning, the mountain-top, the sun, the eagle, volcanic lava, Pegasus, Plato, and God. He was the object of frenetic praise and adoration that verged on megalomania. Trujillo statues, busts, and monuments were erected throughout the country; parks, streets, towns, and mountains were named in his honor; and parades were staged and special masses said for him. Signs and mottos—"Trujillo Forever," at village pumps "Trujillo Gives Us Drink," and in the hospitals "Trujillo Cures Us"—hailed the dictator. Some cynic remarked that it was surprising that God's name appeared first on the famous neon sign "God and Trujillo" which hung over the harbor of the capital. When he appeared in public, Dominicans learned to remove their hats, place them over their hearts, and bow their heads. Professional propagandists—public-relations firms in New York, lobbyists in Washington, and many other paid agents—championed his regime.

During almost the entire Trujillo era, church and state supported each other in a mutually beneficial way. Trujillo granted numerous favors to the Catholic Church and, in 1954, signed a concordat with the Vatican that bestowed even greater concessions; in return, the Church supported his regime. By the same token, the dictator used the Church's praise of him to further his own political ends. By linking it with his own propaganda system and official ideology, he moved further and further toward modern totalitarianism.

In the mid-1950's, however, at precisely the time when Trujillo reached the height of his power, forces began to work that would eventually culminate in his overthrow. First of all, the growing list of fallen Latin American strongmen made the Dominican dictatorship appear anachronistic. As a result, the morale of the opposition to Trujillo was strengthened, and new efforts to topple the dictatorship were stimulated. Secondly, in 1956, Trujillo apparently arranged to have Jesús de Galíndez, an exiled Spaniard and one of his most articulate critics, killed.

Galíndez' doctoral dissertation at Columbia University had been a damning exposé of Trujillo's dictatorship. According to the most widely accepted accounts, Trujillo had him kidnaped off the streets of New York and flown to the Dominican Republic, where he was killed. Galíndez was internationally known, and his murder (as well as that of the American pilot who had flown the fatal mission) caused a storm of protest and attracted enormously unfavorable attention to the Dominican regime.

Trujillo then attempted to overthrow or, that failing, to assassinate another vigorous opponent—President Rómulo Betancourt of Venezuela. On one occasion, Trujillo loaded a plane with anti-Betancourt pamphlets intending to have them scattered over Caracas. But the confused pilot dumped them on Curaçao, a Dutch island off the coast of Venezuela, and then landed on another Dutch island, Aruba, when he ran out of gas. Another time, Trujillo helped to arrange an invasion of Venezuela, which was quickly repulsed, however. The third attempt to kill Betancourt almost succeeded: A planted bomb went off, badly burning the Venezuelan President—but he survived. Trujillo's plots against Betancourt induced the Organization of American States to vote diplomatic and economic sanctions against the Dominican Republic. Sensing an anti-Trujillo trend in Latin America and fearing that the fall of the Cuban dictator Batista and Castro's rise to power might be repeated, the United States, to insure that a "second Cuba" would not occur, began to move against the Dominican dictatorship.

As the external opposition to Trujillo increased, internal opposition grew as well, stimulated by the economic crises that began with the dictator's financially disastrous Peace Fair in 1955, and that continued as prices fell for Dominican products, especially sugar. The financial crisis was accelerated by Trujillo's wild expenditures on arms following an abortive invasion in 1959 launched against his regime by Dominican exiles and others based in Cuba. Important sectors of the business-professional-landholding elite, middle-class merchants, members of the government, the Church, and the armed forces became disenchanted with the regime's corruption and stepped-up terror, and some began to plot its overthrow. On the night of May 30, 1961, en route to a rendezvous with his mistress, Trujillo was brutally assassinated. A monument now marks the spot.

For thirty-one years Trujillo had exercised absolute control over almost all aspects of life in the Dominican Republic. Few Dominicans knew anything but life under Trujillo, and the country was inexperienced in democratic methods and procedures. The political institutions that might have facilitated a peaceful and orderly transition to democracy were almost wholly lacking.

Because near-total control had been concentrated in his hands, the Generalissimo's death produced a near-total vacuum. At the time, Max Frankel, of *The New York Times*, wrote: "The sixty-nine-year-old Generalissimo, who ruled for thirty-one years, left more than a power vacuum in his capital. In the Dominican Republic he has left an ideological void, a people unaccustomed to governing themselves and unschooled in any political doctrine except the jungle doctrine that the strongest shall rule."*

The huge military apparatus, trained in the corrupt and oppressive tactics of the Trujillo era, emerged as the strongest force in the country after the dictator's death and remained largely immune to attempts to reform the society along more democratic lines. Nepotism and corruption prevailed in the government as well. Without experience in the practice of local self-government, in genuine elections, in government by constitution, in the rule of law, in the proper functioning of political parties, and in a wide range of other governmental and political processes, the Dominicans stood little chance of building a functioning democratic system.

Much of the natural wealth of the country had been drained

* June 4, 1961, Sect. IV, p. 4.

off or wastefully used, and the future of the vast Trujillo properties remained uncertain. Agriculture, commerce, and industry —indeed, the entire economy—could not recover from the enormous problems bequeathed by the fallen regime. Similarly, socio-economic groups and associations, which had been tightly controlled by the dictatorship, remained highly divided and unevenly organized after 1961, thus making the integration of the nation nearly impossible. Divisions among social groups and economic classes were often so deep and so bitter that the whole country seemed at times on the verge of collapse.

An entirely new system of values was needed to replace the Trujillo ideology and the cult of the dictator. But this required a complete reform of the educational system and a total change in the media of mass communications. The Church as well had difficulty overcoming the legacy of its long-time close association with the dictatorship, and its attempts to fill the moral, spiritual, and ethical void were not wholly successful.

Because of the U.S.–created constabulary through which Trujillo rose to power; the praise which American congressmen, ambassadors, and other high officials showered upon him; and the close and friendly relationship which for many years existed between the two countries, many Dominicans thought the United States had a share in the blame for the longevity of the dictatorship. To a certain extent, the Communists were able to exploit this apparent alliance between the United States and Trujillo by making the choice appear to be between U.S.–backed Trujilloism on the one hand or Communism on the other. Completely rejecting Trujilloism, most Dominicans preferred other, often radical and revolutionary—sometimes even Communist—alternatives. U.S. efforts in the post-Trujillo years to help direct Dominican developments were made more difficult because of its earlier association with the dictatorship.

The political development and modernization of the country were also interrupted, set back, and perhaps permanently retarded

by the imposition of the Trujillo dictatorship. At a time, therefore, when most of the Latin American countries were, in varying degrees and fashions, making a great leap forward into the
twentieth century, the Dominican Republic remained in the
strait-jacket of perhaps the most nearly totalitarian dictatorship
Latin America had ever known.

Chapter V

AFTER TRUJILLO

THE ORIGINAL PLAN of the conspirators against the Trujillo regime had been to assassinate the dictator, to round up and jail, deport, or kill his closest friends and relatives, and to gain hold of the reins of government. The first goal—the assassination—was successfully accomplished, but the other aims could not be carried out because of several unexpected developments. (For example, the conspirator who was responsible for rounding up members of Trujillo's family had been sent on a mission out of the capital by the Generalissimo himself, and, rather than risking suspicion, he carried out Trujillo's order, with the result that the Trujillo family went unharmed.) The failure of the conspirators' entire plan to function smoothly paved the way for the chaos and revolution of the succeeding post-Trujillo years rather than for a peaceful and orderly transfer of power.

The Trujillo dictatorship, then, did not collapse with the assassination of the Generalissimo on the night of May 30, 1961. Instead, power continued in the hands of President Joaquín Balaguer, a puppet of the slain dictator, and, more importantly, in the hands of Trujillo's son and heir apparent Rafael Jr. (Ramfis), who controlled the armed forces. Though Balaguer was in nominal charge of the government, it was clear that the Trujillo family made all important decisions, and the apparatus of the old dictatorship remained intact.

Those who inherited the slain Trujillo's mantle had neither

his ability nor his inclination. Balaguer, a weak and ineffectual individual, was uncomfortable in his position. Ramfis was a carouser and playboy who was happier chasing Hollywood starlets than exercising the responsibilities of power. Most important, however, Trujillo's system of absolute personal control over the country had not prepared any group or person, including his son, to fill his shoes. The dictatorship began almost immediately to disintegrate.

The ruling Trujillos were caught on the horns of several dilemmas which they were unable to resolve. On the one hand, the economic sanctions imposed by the Organization of American States (OAS) and buttressed by the United States' cutting of the Dominican Republic's sugar quota remained in effect. On the other, the groups—businessmen, professionals, and landholders—who had plotted to assassinate Trujillo now pressured Ramfis to end the excesses of the dictatorship and have the sanctions lifted.

Cautiously, Ramfis began to instigate a few reforms. For not only did the sanctions hurt the business elements, but they also diminished the profits of the Trujillos, the country's chief proprietors. In a series of moves to get the sanctions lifted, Ramfis began to curb police brutality, turned some of the family's wealth over to the people, forced out some of the most hated cohorts of the former regime, including two of his uncles, and allowed the formation of opposition movements.

This "democratization" of the dictatorship, however, impaled the regime on another horn of the dilemma. By allowing an opposition to form, the Trujillo family threatened its own long-secure position. And that opposition, ever more powerful and vociferous, insisted that the economic sanctions remain in effect until *all* the Trujillos had left the country. Furthermore, the United States was exerting heavy pressure on the Balaguer-Ramfis government behind the scenes.

For nearly six months, an uneasy balance was maintained

among these contending pressures. In November, 1961, the situation came to a climax. The United States, in response to the limited reforms the government had made, suggested to the OAS that *some* of the sanctions against the Dominican Republic be lifted. The Trujillos, however, feeling they had lived up to their end of the bargain, thought that *all* the sanctions should be lifted and accused the United States of doublecrossing them. The slain dictator's two exiled brothers—Héctor and Arismendi—were especially infuriated. They felt that Ramfis had already given away too much of the family fortune and was jeopardizing continued Trujillo rule by permitting the growth of the opposition. As his two uncles hurried home from exile in nearby Bermuda, Ramfis abruptly resigned as chief of the armed forces and fled the country. Before leaving, however, he had many of those who had earlier been arrested for the killing of his father summarily shot.

Ramfis' resignation left a power vacuum in the Dominican Republic which the Trujillo brothers now attempted to fill. Because of the imminent threat of the re-establishment of an absolute dictatorship and the elimination of even the most limited of the recent reforms, coupled with the fear that the situation might degenerate into chaos and that the Communists might step into the vacuum, the United States sent a portion of its Atlantic fleet to maneuver three miles off Santo Domingo, thus manifesting its opposition to the Trujillos. Powerful elements in the Dominican armed forces also refused to go along with the Trujillo brothers' power grab and declared their allegiance to President Balaguer. Confronted with such opposition, the Trujillos capitulated. On November 20, 1961, Héctor and Arismendi, together with other members of the family and their associates, boarded a chartered Pan American plane and flew into exile. The Trujillo era had finally come to an end after thirty-one years.

With the Trujillos gone, Balaguer now became president of

the Dominican Republic in deed as well as in word. Most Dominicans, however, needed some time to realize that the end of the dictatorship was not just a hoax. Then the capital erupted in wild victory celebrations which lasted for a week. Mobs looted the many Trujillo mansions (some Dominican families simply moved into the houses and are still there) and sought revenge against agents of the dictatorship who had not yet fled the country. Santo Domingo became a forest of headless statues, as the rampaging populace destroyed the many monuments to the Generalissimo. Car owners painted out the "Era of Trujillo" motto on their license plates. By the end of the week, the most visible reminders of the hated Trujillo regime were gone.

The populace next turned on President Balaguer himself. Balaguer had, after all, been a Trujillo puppet; and though he had managed to stay aloof from the worst atrocities of the dictatorship, he was considered a *trujillista*. Only one week after the Trujillos had left the country, the National Civic Union (UCN), a civic-patriotic opposition group formed shortly after Trujillo's death, launched a general strike—the first in the nation's history —to oust Balaguer from the presidency. Though the strike failed to achieve its immediate goal, it galvanized public opinion and clearly demonstrated the people's sentiment.

Balaguer sought to counter this opposition and cultivate a popular following of his own by giving away some of the vast Trujillo properties, which the government had inherited. But his efforts to stay in power were not sufficient. The opposition continued to pressure him to step down. When, finally, the United States gave its support to the opposition, Balaguer was persuaded to share power with a Council of State.

The seven-man Council took office on January 1, 1962. It was composed of Balaguer (who continued as president), three prominent business and professional men who had been active in the opposition, a priest who had gained notoriety by standing up to Trujillo, and the only two survivors of the group that had assassinated Trujillo. It was felt that the inclusion of these men in the government would make it more representative.

The major power in the country, however, remained in the hands of the huge military apparatus that Trujillo had created. After Ramfis' departure, General Pedro Rodríguez Echavarría became chief of the armed forces and it soon became apparent that he had political ambitions. The Council of State had been in office only sixteen days when Rodríguez staged a *coup d'état.* Balaguer was forced to resign and took refuge in the residence of the papal nuncio, while the other Council members (the Trujillo assassins excepted) and the major political party leaders were imprisoned. Rodríguez then set up his own civil-military junta. Huberto Bogaert was appointed chief of state, though there was little doubt that the real authority was exercised by the chief of the armed forces.

The reactions to this coup, in the Dominican Republic and in Washington, were almost entirely negative. Businesses closed in protest, judges resigned, government employees refused to work, students rioted, and the United States cut off all promised aid. In the face of these protests, Rodríguez went to the key San Isidro air force base to negotiate with the imprisoned Council members. Upon his arrival, air force officers placed him, their own commander, under arrest and freed the councilmen. Rodríguez Echavarría's rule had lasted only forty-eight hours.

Soon he was sent into exile, and the Council of State was reinstated. Rafael Bonnelly moved up to the presidency, replacing Balaguer (who was also sent into exile); Donald J. Reid Cabral was appointed the seventh member of the Council. This Council ruled for the next thirteen months, until the inauguration of a new administration on February 27, 1963.

The most important objective of this interim government was to preside over an orderly and peaceful transition from the Trujillo dictatorship to a democratic and constitutional system. The Council managed to stay in power—not so simple a task, given the enormous problems facing it—to arrange for and hold free elections, and to step down peacefully when the elected government was installed. With respect to its primary aim, then, the Council was eminently successful. In other matters, however, its accomplishments were limited.

A new era in Dominican history began with the installation of this second Council. The worst of the *trujillistas* were by this time out of the country. Freedom and liberty were now manifest in nearly all aspects of Dominican life. The former Trujillo properties were held by the government as part of the national patrimony. The United States, in addition, began to pour in enormous amounts of money, manpower, and technical aid in an effort to help the Council master the difficulties of transition. U.S. per-capita aid to the Dominican Republic reached a higher level at that time than in any other Latin American country, and a number of international organizations also began to tackle the country's many problems.

Political activity also flourished. A number of political parties came into existence to vie in the forthcoming election. The communications media became free, critical, and educational. First attempts were made to launch a non-Communist agrarian reform and to integrate the traditionally forgotten peasantry into the national life. Several independent labor organizations began to speak for, educate, and organize the workers. Business and professional associations were formed. The government workers were no longer harassed and persecuted as they had been during the Trujillo dictatorship. The Church came out publicly in favor of democracy and social reform. And an effort was also made to reorient the armed forces along democratic lines.

The problems that the Dominican Republic had to overcome if it was to achieve a functioning democratic system were enormous. About 40 per cent of the working force was unemployed, and the economy was stagnant. The government was unable to control the mobs in the streets. The new political parties and interest groups were still weak, and the country had no practice in democratic government. The Council made some notable efforts to resolve the difficult problems bequeathed it by thirty-one years of Trujillo's absolutism. It kept the Trujillo properties despite attempts by many international carpetbaggers to make a fast buck at the nation's expense. It succeeded in establishing a degree of law and order. It warded off attacks from the Communists and the Castro-oriented left, which called for a revolution and thought that the Council was proceeding too slowly, as well as from the right, which thought that even its limited reforms were "Communistic."

Some of the problems the Council faced were insoluble—as, for example, the need to "de-Trujilloize" the public service. To oust all those who had collaborated with the Trujillos would have meant the dismissal of almost the entire bureaucracy, leaving no one capable of running the machinery of government. The nature of Trujillo's system meant that, in one fashion or another, nearly everyone was a collaborator. A wholesale purge would have been disastrous for the already undermanned and talent-short public service.

Not only was the Council limited in what it could achieve; it was even more restricted by what it sought to accomplish. The Council and the rest of the government hierarchy were dominated by business-professional elements and members of the Dominican Republic's traditional ruling families—men who were not prepared to enact the sorely needed economic, social, and political reforms which would lead to a democratic system. They therefore refused to carry out, in more than a token way, measures that would result in a more equitable sharing of the nation's wealth and would be detrimental to the oligarchy's own interests. The agrarian-reform program, for example, received much publicity, but little land was actually deeded to the peasants.

Despite its often dedicated and sincere efforts to steer the country in new directions and to help erase Trujillo's legacy, the

Council did not gain widespread support and was never very popular. As its term wore on, it became increasingly unrepresentative as well. The largest political party was not represented on it, and the emerging labor and peasant sectors had no say in matters that affected them. The Council's contacts with the people were confined to an occasional television appearance or dedication ceremony. Its programs failed to evoke a favorable response even from those who benefited from them, and the over-all impression was that the country tolerated the Council only because no one could think of a better alternative.

The negative impact of the Council was a major factor in the outcome of the scheduled elections. Several Council members were closely associated with the increasingly conservative National Civic Union, headed by Viriato Fiallo, a well-meaning but colorless physician. This identification of the UCN and the Council (which earned the former the damning epithet "Party of the Rich") became an albatross for Fiallo, now a candidate for president, and for the UCN in general. Many Dominicans, especially in the lower classes, where the election would be decided, condemned the Council as a group of do-nothings and felt that Fiallo's election would only perpetuate inaction.

Still, the Council did succeed in bringing off the first free elections in thirty-eight years and in handing over political authority to the new government. Several pre-election crises nearly torpedoed these efforts, but the Council survived them all. The major task of building a democratic society, however, remained to be accomplished.

The elections of December 20, 1962, were won by Juan Bosch and his Dominican Revolutionary Party (PRD). Bosch, a writer and intellectual, had left the Dominican Republic early in the Trujillo era, had organized his reform-oriented party in exile, and had returned to his country only in 1961. He was considered free of compromising ties with the Dominican oligarchy and the hated Trujillo regime. Bosch was a purist in other respects, too:

He was an idealist, a teacher, and a moralist. His was a humanistic rather than a pragmatic approach to politics, and he thought of himself as a prophet whose mission was to transform his country. Bosch came to office with a philosophy of government based on a belief in absolute justice, absolute honesty, absolute freedom, and absolute democracy.

Bosch carried the hopes of most Dominicans with him into office. In an election that most observers thought would be very close, he won the presidency by a two to one vote, and the PRD won comparable majorities in both houses of Congress. Bosch interpreted this victory as a mandate to build a free and democratic nation on the ruins of the fallen dictatorship. His overwhelming electoral triumph was construed by the PRD leadership as a vote against privileged interests, government favoritism, and high-level corruption and for the initiation of a peaceful revolution.

Bosch promised not only political liberty but social and economic democracy as well. "I belong to the family of democratic revolutionary parties," he said. "We are democratic because we want to preserve and expand political freedoms. We are revolutionary because we want to initiate a society of justice." He promised a wide range of reforms and intended to bring about fundamental transformations in the social, economic, and political life of the Dominican Republic. Although the PRD's platform demanded freedom for all sectors of society, it was partial to traditionally underprivileged groups such as labor and the peasantry.

The greatest electoral support for Bosch, indeed, had come from these same lower-class elements. The PRD had been established, after all, as a peasants' and workers' organization, and Bosch was known as the candidate of the "have-nots." He heaped venom upon his richer and aristocratic opponents—whom he called *tutempotes* (a Dominican expression meaning "big shots"). Class lines were thus tightly drawn.

The obstacles that Bosch had to surmount if he was to lead the Dominican Republic to full democracy were huge. For more than three decades the Dominican people had been held in the bondage of the Trujillo tyranny. This had been followed by a year of only limited reforms under the transitional Council of State. Thus, Bosch aimed at establishing democracy in a country where few knew or remembered democratic practices. His tasks included a revitalization of the stagnant economy, the warding off of attacks from both left and right, getting enough capable technicians to carry out his ambitious programs, the education of the many illiterates, the development of industry, the improvement and diversification of agriculture, the establishment of civilian control over the military, the strengthening of peasant and labor organizations, the mollification of the many dangerously divisive forces in the country. All these major tasks—and more—had to be accomplished if a genuinely democratic system were to be established.

Immediately after his election, Bosch traveled to the United States, where he conferred with President Kennedy and Alliance for Progress officials. He then went to Europe and arranged for additional economic aid. Although he was received with a tumultuous welcome upon his return to the Dominican Republic, the seeds of discontent had already been planted. Conservative groups were already conspiring against him, and they icily rejected his invitation to join a national unity government and work for the betterment of the entire country. To make matters worse, Bosch needlessly antagonized some of his powerful opponents by making several cantankerous statements before he was even inaugurated. Despite these ominous forebodings, Bosch was inaugurated on February 27, 1963, with the hopes of most Dominicans, of many Latin Americans, and of the United States Government riding on his shoulders.

At first, Bosch attempted to smooth over the antagonisms that had been generated in the election campaign and to allay the fears of those who felt threatened by his proposed revolutionary programs. He demonstrated fiscal conservatism to the business community, avoided tampering with the sensitive armed forces, and tried to conciliate his opponents in the oligarchy and the Church. At the same time, however, Bosch began to carry out his revolutionary programs. As these programs unfolded, the latent opposition to him grew. He antagonized some members of U.S. missions by failing to endorse various Alliance for Progress objectives and by asserting a more independent attitude than the Council or the Trujillo governments had ever shown. Other American officials became disillusioned with what they now viewed as Bosch's ineffective leadership. His attempts to change the traditional behavior patterns in the bureaucracy alienated the civil servants. His new constitution did not recognize Catholicism as the state religion and thus drew the criticism of the Church hierarchy. The peasants were mobilized, and a revitalized agrarian-reform program was launched. This frightened landowning and military elements, who accused him of creating a militia like the one in Castro's Cuba. Favoritism to labor, together with vague references in the new constitution concerning private-property rights, gained Bosch the opposition of employers and businessmen.

The issue that united the most powerful opposition groups was the alleged growth of Communism in the Dominican Republic. In accordance with his conception of a democratic society, the President allowed absolute freedom for all political groups, including the Communists. Some elements in the Church, the armed forces, and the business-professional-landholding elite were in agreement that the government's policies would result in the transformation of the Dominican Republic into another Cuba. Though there was actually no likelihood that the weak and feuding Communist factions might or could take over, the conservatives *believed* that a Castro-like revolution was imminent. In the face of this increased opposition to his rule, Bosch refused to compromise on his principles and did nothing to alleviate these fears or conciliate the only sectors in the society that had the power to oust him.

On September 25, 1963, after only seven months in office, Bosch and his government were overthrown in a coup staged by the armed forces and actively supported by some clerics and much of the oligarchy. Bosch and the principal PRD officials were sent into exile, and the party headquarters and its affiliated labor and peasant organizations were raided and closed down. The "Showcase for the Alliance for Progress" became a broken and empty shopwindow. Most important, the Dominican Republic's attempt to bridge the transition from the Trujillo dictatorship to a political, economic, and social democracy was severely set back.

Immediately after Bosch's ouster, the armed forces turned power over to a civilian Triumvirate headed by Emilio de los Santos. The UCN-dominated Triumvirate government was staffed with members of the same elite families whom Bosch had beaten two to one in the election nine months earlier. Several attempts were made by PRD leaders to force a return to constitutional government, but they were rejected by the Dominican Republic's new rulers. Without effective leadership, the country began to drift toward chaos.

The initial climax to this degenerative period came in December, when a small group of pro-Castro guerrillas was slaughtered by armed forces elements after it had surrendered. The incident so shocked President de los Santos, whose nephew had been one of those killed, that he resigned. Corruption, terrorism, and oppression soon became even more widespread. The society disintegrated to the point where a complete breakdown seemed imminent; the Dominican Republic's political system came to resemble not a single unified nation but a pattern of hateful, warring subnations.

The two remaining Triumvirate members, after conferring

with military and political leaders, picked Donald Reid Cabral to replace de los Santos as president. Under Reid, several halting steps were taken to lift the country up again, and he did his best to effect a revitalization of the national economy. The U.S. aid program, suspended upon Bosch's ouster, was resumed. Though himself of the elite, Reid began a new agrarian-reform program—which, however, consisted largely of handing out worthless land titles to the *campesinos*—and initiated a number of other limited reforms for the benefit of the lower classes. Reid also enforced a needed austerity drive and took steps to reduce the rampant corruption (mostly in the armed forces, whose members imported goods duty-free through their tax-exempt canteens and resold them to the public on the black market). Reid permitted all political parties (the several Communist groups excepted) to carry on their activities, and promised to hold new national elections. Lastly, he purged the armed forces of some of their most corrupt and oppressive elements left over from Trujillo's days.

It was precisely at this moment of moderate upswing and of slow, gradual improvement that the bloody and chaotic revolution of April, 1965, broke out. It seems ironic that Reid, who belonged to the oligarchy and had been chosen for the presidency with the military's approval, was ousted by the armed forces at least partially because of the reforms he had initiated. These reforms had particularly angered certain elements in the armed forces, who, determined to protect their special privileges, wanted to rid themselves of Reid but were also steadfastly opposed to Bosch's resumption of power.

Despite the reforms he had begun, it should not be thought that Reid was a very popular figure. In the eyes of the PRD leadership, he represented the oligarchy and those who had overthrown the constitutional government. From the point of view of the PRD's followers, Reid was responsible for the terrorism (party sympathizers were frequently jailed and beaten), the oppression (pro-Bosch groups were often persecuted), and the corruption (his efforts to eliminate the canteen "companies" had not been successful) that had not existed during Bosch's democratic administration. Furthermore, Reid apparently planned to emerge triumphant from the scheduled 1965 presidential election by prohibiting the more popular candidates, Bosch and Balaguer, from entering the country, and by carefully controlling the balloting. Moreover, at a time of rising prices for such basic foodstuffs as rice and beans, the day-in, day-out staples of the poor, Reid's austerity program demanded a freeze on wages: the brunt of the suffering was borne by the poor. For many Dominicans of virtually all classes (including many business-men, who could not compete with the military black market and who, ironically, began to wish for Bosch's return), the Reid government remained unpopular, uncharismatic, unrepresenta-tive, and illegitimate.

The revolution that began on April 24, 1965, was launched by those who, for diverse reasons, were opposed to Reid's continu-ance in the presidency. It became a civil war when these reasons proved irreconcilable: some simply wanted to get rid of Reid, others wanted also to return Bosch to power. The latter, the "Constitutionalist" group, made up of both civilian and military men, installed Rafael Molina Ureña as president and seemed on the verge of defeating the anti-Bosch military junta, led officially by Colonel Pedro Bartolomé Benoit and in fact by General Elías Wessin y Wessin, the head of the armed forces training school. It was at this point that the United States intervened.

Fearing that a victory by the Constitutionalists might turn the Dominican Republic into a "second Cuba," the United States landed a contingent of troops in the country which eventually numbered more than 20,000 men. The U.S. action bolstered the unpopular junta forces and probably prevented the pro-Bosch elements from coming to power. The United States was also instrumental in setting up a Government of National Reconstruction under Antonio Imbert, one of Trujillo's assassins. In the meantime, a U.S. proposal for the creation of an Inter-American Peace Force composed of the U.S. forces already in the Dominican Republic plus military units from Brazil, Nicaragua, Honduras, Paraguay (all of them more or less dictatorships), and tiny Costa Rica, was approved by the Organization of American States.

For this military intervention in a small and weak but supposedly sovereign nation, and for its alignment on the side of reactionary elements and against popular forces, the United States was severely criticized at home and abroad. Because of the deliberately misleading information the administration gave to the public, the outright lies in which government spokesmen were caught, and the fantastic blunders and incompetence associated with the entire operation, many observers felt that President Johnson's "credibility gap" as well as his difficulties with informed opinion-makers in the United States and elsewhere should be traced initially not so much to the Viet-Nam war as to the Dominican intervention.

Eventually, the armed conflict between the Constitutionalists, under the leadership of Colonel Francisco Caamaño, and the Imbert government was reduced to a stalemate. The United States, meanwhile, began to search for a middle-of-the-road compromise government. On September 3, 1965, a provisional government under Héctor García Godoy, a member of one of the country's most prominent families and for a time Secretary of Foreign Relations in the Bosch government, was inaugurated. However, being a compromise arrangement, the García Godoy administration was not fully accepted by either right or left and came under fire from both sides. The right attacked García Godoy for including some Constitutionalists in the government whom the conservatives considered "Communist"; and the left criticized it for not instigating sufficient reforms or curbing the power of the armed forces. At the same time, the economy was near collapse; hatred and bitterness were still intense; and the continued presence of U.S. and Latin American troops, which many Dominicans considered to be an occupation force, further aggravated the situation.

During García Godoy's provisional presidency, none of the basic problems that had caused the revolution to break out in the first place were solved. García Godoy apparently saw himself as a mediator among the contending Dominican factions and not as an effective and forceful leader. His government managed to survive—and little else. In a sense, his interim presidency was like the interim rule of the Council of State during 1962—moderate, conciliatory, and concerned mainly with survival until elections could bring about a constitutionally elected government. Frequently, his term in office was rocky, as in December, 1965, when the Constitutionalists and so-called "loyalist" military forces clashed again, and on several occasions he narrowly missed being overthrown. On the other hand García Godoy managed to reduce some of the tensions generated by the 1965 revolution and civil war, and the country began to prepare for new elections on June 1, 1966.

The leading contenders were now Balaguer and Bosch, and the campaign between them was unique in many respects. The two candidates were personal friends, and in his campaign pronouncements Bosch consistently praised Balaguer as a fine man. Yet, most of their followers considered them diametrically opposed: Balaguer, the symbol of peace, tranquility, and the status quo; Bosch, the symbol of revolution, Constitutionalism, and social change. The contest between the two seemingly polarized forces was acrimonious and sometimes violent; a campaign of systematic terrorism was launched against PRD officials and Bosch followers in the countryside. Since he feared assassination and realized that the terror in the countryside was particularly directed against him, Bosch remained in his house and limited his speech-making mostly to radio broadcasts. Balaguer, by contrast, traveled and spoke throughout the nation, ran a well-financed and very skillful race, and was particularly clever in winning votes among women and peasants. Many Dominicans, apparently tired of bloodshed and constant upheaval, voted for Balaguer, fearing that a Bosch victory might mean continued revolution and chaos. In what was generally conceded to be a fairly honest election (the Bosch supporters dispute this), Balaguer and his Partido Reformista won a surprisingly easy victory.

Balaguer was inaugurated on July 1, 1966. Though it is still too early to assess his government with any degree of certainty, Balaguer's first moves as president were moderate and conciliatory. The constitution promulgated by his government combined the better features of former Dominican constitutions. It was reformist in its orientation but couched in noninflammatory terms and it remained silent on many controversial issues that had previously torn the country apart. Balaguer's limited reform proposals were designed to assure the loyalty of the conservatives, while his gradual curtailment of the power of the military was generally applauded by the reform-minded groups. He reduced the salaries of government officials and instigated a strict austerity program; but he sought to balance these moves by slashing electricity rates and ordering price cuts on basic foodstuffs. He appointed leftists as well as rightists to various posts, which kept his opponents divided and off-balance, and he was able to recruit some prominent members of Bosch's party to serve in the government, thereby making it more broadly based and lending a feeling of national unity. The United States, meanwhile, sought to bolster the economy with massive infusions of aid and to rebuild what had been destroyed during the revolution. A large variety of development projects was initiated.

Though Balaguer was undoubtedly a skilled and clever politician, willing, for example, to retreat from an unpopular position, he was also fortunate in having a loyal and democratic opposition and in receiving the political benefits that accrued from the withdrawal of the Inter-American Peace Force and the restoration of national sovereignty. Furthermore, there remained considerable doubt as to whether Balaguer, with all his political acumen and with massive U.S. assistance behind him, was making more than a minor dent in the country's immense problems. His government seemed to rest on a foundation firmer than that of his predecessors; but this foundation was still very tenuous, and the quicksands of Dominican politics could at almost any time cause the entire edifice to collapse.

The following chronology should help to clarify for the reader the succession of post-Trujillo governments.

A Chronology of Post-Trujillo Governments

1. Joaquín Balaguer, President. August 2, 1960–December 31, 1961*
2. Council of State. January 1, 1962. Dissolved by military coup, January 16, 1962.
    > Joaquín Balaguer, President
    > Rafael F. Bonnelly, First Vice President
    > Eduardo Read Barreras, Second Vice President
    > Nicolás Pichardo
    > Msgr. Eliseo Pérez Sánchez
    > Luís Amiama Tió
    > Antonio Imbert Barrera
3. Civilian-Military Junta. January 16, 1962. Replaced by Council of State, January 18, 1962.
    > Huberto Bogaert, President
    > Armando Oscar Pacheco
    > Luís Amiama Tió
    > Antonio Imbert Barrera

---

* From the time of the assassination of the dictator Trujillo until November, 1961, Balaguer shared power with Lt. Gen. Rafael L. Trujillo, Jr. ("Ramfis"), who was head of the armed forces. After the departure of Ramfis on November 18, Balaguer retained at least nominal control until the installation of the first Council of State.

R. Adm. Enrique Váldez Vidaurre
Maj. Wilfredo Medina Natalio
Col. Neit R. Nivar Seijas
4. Council of State. January 18, 1962. Replaced by Bosch Government, February 27, 1963.
>Rafael F. Bonnelly, President
Eduardo Read Barreras, First Vice President*
Nicolás Pichardo, Second Vice President
Msgr. Eliseo Pérez Sánchez
Luís Amiama Tió
Antonio Imbert Barrera
Donald Reid Cabral
5. Constitutional Government. February 27, 1963. Overthrown by *coup d'état*, September 25, 1963.
>Juan Bosch, President
Segundo Armando González Tamayo, Vice President
6. Triumvirate. September 26, 1963. Overthrown by *coup d'état*, April 25, 1965.
>Emilio de los Santos, President. Resigned December 22, 1963; replaced by Donald Reid Cabral
Ramón Tapia Espinal. Resigned April 9, 1964; replaced by Ramón Cáceres Troncoso
Manuel E. Taváres Espaillat. Resigned June 27, 1964; not replaced.
7. Civil war. April 25, 1965–August 31, 1965.
>"Constitutional" Government. April 25–August 31, 1965.
>>José Rafael Molina Ureña, Acting President (April 25–27)
Col. Francisco Caamaño Deño, President (May 4–August 31)
>Military Junta. April 27–May 7, 1965.
>>Col. Pedro Bartolomé Benoit, President
Col. Enrique Apolinario Casado Saladin
Capt. Manuel Santana Carasco
>"Government of National Reconstruction." May 7–August 30, 1965.
>>Brig. Gen. Antonio Imbert Barrera, President
Julio D. Postigo
Carlos Grisolia Poloney
Alejandro Zeller Cocco
Col. Pedro Bartolomé Benoit

---

* Upon the resignation of Read Barreras in February, 1962, Pichardo became First Vice President, Reid Cabral became Second Vice President, and José Fernández Caminero was named to fill the vacancy.

8. Provisional Government. September 3, 1965. Replaced by Balaguer Government, July 1, 1966.

      Héctor García Godoy, Provisional President

9. Constitutional Government, July 1, 1966.

      Joaquín Balaguer, President

      Francisco Augusto Lora, Vice President

Chapter VI

THE PEOPLE

IN COMPARISON to the peoples of many developing countries, the Dominican population is, in certain respects, fairly uniform and homogeneous. Almost all Dominicans practice the same religion—Catholicism—and speak the same language—Spanish. They take pride in the same Latin-Hispanic culture and share many of the same values and patterns of behavior. Even racially there is a degree of uniformity. Though some are white and others Negro, the great majority of Dominicans are mulattoes. A problem that has impeded national development in many emerging countries, namely that of two or more cultures, tribes, language or ethnic groups existing side by side within a single nation but with no contact or interchange between them, is not of great importance in the Dominican Republic.

And yet, the Dominican Republic's 3.5 million people do not form a highly integrated nation. They share certain characteristics but this does not mean that they are united. Despite a common language, a common religion, a common cultural and behavioral make-up, and even a common racial "melting pot," Dominicans exhibit little solidarity. Indeed, the fact that the Dominican Republic is a highly divided and deeply fissured nation—socially, economically, and politically—helps to explain why it has not been able to achieve a stable and workable governmental system.

ETHNIC GROUPS

Three major racial strains are fused in the Dominican people —the Indian, the European, and the Negro. In more recent decades, other ethnic groups have settled in the Dominican Republic.

The Indian strain is today the least important of the three. When Columbus and his men landed on Hispaniola, the Caribs, a marauding cannibal tribe that had originated in South America and had conquered its way up from the Lesser to the Greater Antilles (and for whom the Caribbean Sea is named), were preying on the peaceable and pastoral Tainos (or Arawaks) who had previously settled on the island. It was the Caribs who wiped out the first Spanish settlement, which in turn led the Spaniards to retaliate against all tribes.

The conquistadors were eager to find gold and glory. In their quest, the Indians were often inhumanly treated, for the Spaniards slaughtered and enslaved them. Even more Indians died from diseases carried by the Spaniards, for which the Indians had no immunity. (The Indians apparently got their revenge, however. Syphilis was endemic among them, and it is believed that this disease was carried from Hispaniola to the rest of the world.)

No one knows how large the indigenous population of Hispaniola was in 1492; estimates range from 300,000 to 3 million. Whatever the original number (the smaller figure is probably more accurate), there is no doubt that most were quickly killed or died in great numbers. A census in 1508 estimated the survivors at 60,000; by 1550, the Indians had been all but completely wiped out. Subsequent Dominican history therefore involves the intermingling of two and not three races.

Few traces remain of Hispaniola's native inhabitants. Indian relics can still be found, waiters in hotels may be dressed as Caribs or Tainos for the benefit of the tourists, and some of the

Indian heroes are romantically glorified in Dominican art and literature, as, for example, *Enriquillo*, the classic Dominican novel by Manuel de Jesús Galván that tells the story of the last Indian chief resisting the Spanish conquerors. During the early decades of Spanish rule, miscegenation between Europeans and Indians and between Negroes and Indians was widespread, and Dominican anthropologists point to this as evidence for the "mestizoness" of today's population. But the Dominican Republic is not like Mexico, Guatemala, Ecuador, Peru, or Bolivia, where Indian and white civilizations—and hence a dualism in language, religion, culture, and traditions—continue to exist even today. The indigenous population of Hispaniola either disappeared or was absorbed by other racial elements. Indian influence in today's Dominican Republic is negligible.

To replace the Indians, whom they had relied on as a work force, the Spaniards imported African slaves. (While slavery should not be condoned, it may be important to remember that at this time the question whether Indians and Africans had souls was the subject of vigorous debate.) As early as 1503, Africans were used to mine gold, and, thereafter, they were brought in increasing numbers to do all forms of manual labor. By the end of the eighteenth century, the Negro population in the Spanish portion of Hispaniola outnumbered the whites by about two to one.

In contrast to the Indians, the Negroes proved more able to survive hardship. Furthermore, a slave could buy his freedom under Spanish law, and as Spain's rule came to an end, the number of Negro and mulatto freedmen outnumbered both whites and slaves. Although there was little public mingling between whites and Negroes, race relations were freer and easier than in most slave societies. Even today, racial prejudice, as it is known in the United States, is almost nonexistent in the Dominican Republic.

Though the Negro strain was, unlike the Indian, a lasting one, few vestiges of African culture remain. Near the Haitian border, African religious rituals are still practiced; but legacies of African traditions are seldom found in the rest of the Dominican Republic. The habits, beliefs, or life-styles of the African Negroes, like those of the native Indians, were almost completely assimilated into the dominant white European, that is, Spanish, culture.

The Europeans who settled in Hispaniola reflected the society from which they came. In 1492, there was only the Catholic Church, and freedom of religion was unknown. The social structure was based on a feudal, contractual system in which each class, caste, and sector had its separate juridical duties and rights. The scientific revolution, ushered in with the empiricism of Galileo and Newton, had not yet occurred, and education was based upon "revealed truth" and authority. The economy was centered upon the ownership of land—capitalism had not yet taken root in Spain. Traditions of representative or democratic government were also lacking, and the political system was characterized by an authoritarian hierarchy. The practices, institutions, and values carried by the Spaniards to the New World were essentially feudal and pre-modern; many of them continue to exist today in only slightly modified form.

The whites were not numerically a large group. The original conquistadors were badly outnumbered by the Indians; yet, they were able to defeat the original inhabitants within a single decade. Eventually, the whites were also outnumbered by the Negroes, and during the first half of the nineteenth century, most Europeans were driven out or killed by the invading Haitians. A succession of new immigrations from Spain and the Canary Islands helped to redress the racial imbalance.

Though they were always a numerical minority, the Europeans imposed their customs and institutions on the country. In politics, society, economy, and religion—indeed in all respects —Spaniards and Creoles were dominant; and the European culture that they carried to the New World absorbed or snuffed out whatever was left of Indian or Negro culture. Even today Dominican writers are fond of stressing that theirs are the most unadulterated of Old World Spanish customs remaining in the Western Hemisphere, and they make strong efforts to preserve them.

Though the Latin-Hispanic traditions and institutions of the whites predominate, after centuries of racial amalgamation the mulattoes have become the largest group. According to official government census figures, 28.1 per cent of the Dominican population is white, 11.5 per cent Negro, and 60.4 per cent mulatto. By U.S. criteria, however, the percentage of Negroes and mulattoes would be higher and the percentage of pure whites far less. This disparity is explained by the fact that in the United States a man who is one-fourth or one-eighth Negro is considered a Negro; in the Dominican Republic, he would be likely to be considered white.

There are isolated pockets of other peoples scattered around the country. In Samaná, for example, live the English-speaking descendants of former slaves from Baltimore and Philadelphia who sought refuge on Hispaniola in the early nineteenth century. At Sosúa, on the north coast, there is a settlement of Jewish refugees from Europe who came during the 1930's. Their number has decreased from about 125 to 25 families, and they remain famous for the manufacture of sausage and cheese.

In the cities, the Chinese appear to run almost all bars and restaurants, and Lebanese and other Middle Easterners (all indiscriminately called *Turcos*) own many businesses. Near Constanza is a colony of Japanese farmers. Toward the east are some English-speaking coloreds from Jamaica and other islands in the Caribbean settled by the British; while in the western border areas, Haitians have settled. There are many U.S. Government officials, but since comparatively few U.S. private concerns have extensive business dealings in the Dominican Republic, the permanent American community is not large.

Though the country's ruling elite is almost exclusively white, and though darker-skinned people are usually found at the lower end of the social scale, prejudice is more social and economic than racial. A person who is wealthy, comes from a good family, and is well educated is ordinarily accepted in almost all Dominican circles, regardless of his color. Those who are not only Negro but also poor, uneducated, and not wellborn find acceptability severely limited.

Nevertheless some racial prejudice does exist. In small rural communities, anthropologists have found that the lines between different mulatto shades are sharply drawn with little mingling between them. Physical characteristics involving hair, lips, nose, and so forth—as well as color—are used by Dominicans to differentiate fairly sharply among several racial types. Dominicans may thus be referred to not only as *negros, blancos,* or *mulatos* but also as *indios, morenos,* or *prietos.* There is also a rural-urban differentiation according to race—city-dwellers are, by and large, lighter than the rural population. Further, the civilian leadership (ordinarily white) tends to look down on the military elite (who often come from rural, middle-class environments and are hence usually darker). Prejudice against such foreign groups as the Chinese and Japanese, who organized their own vigilante system after several unhappy experiences with nationalistic Dominican justice, also surfaces from time to time.

Throughout Dominican history, emphasis has been placed upon "whitening" oneself, one's descendants (through marriage), and the Dominican population as a whole. Trujillo tried to "lighten" the population by encouraging European immigration and settling the immigrants in remote colonization projects (such as along the Haitian border). Even today, as a result, in predominantly Negro or mulatto areas, one may see a blond with blue eyes. Dominican women, furthermore, often use large amounts of cosmetics in order to appear "whiter." In terms of race, then, the Dominicans are in the majority a mulatto people who think of themselves and would like to be known as white and European. The Dominicans thus look down upon the neighboring Haitians whom they consider Negro, African, and uncivilized.

Such prejudice as does exist in the Dominican Republic, however, is not based on intense racial hatred and separateness, as it is in some other countries. Prejudice is more of a social phenomenon; and skin color and physical characteristics provide only one criteria among several—education, wealth, family background, and so forth—by which one's place in society is determined. In fact, the Dominican Republic has remained remarkably free of racial antagonism.

LANGUAGES

Spanish is the national language of the Dominican Republic, and it is spoken by nearly everyone except the most recent immigrants. Dominican Spanish, as written by the educated, does not differ greatly from the Spanish of other countries, though there exist taboo words, expressions (such as *tutempote* for "big shots"), and shades of meaning that are particularly Dominican. Except in a few regions, the spoken language is clear and easy to understand. There are no language bars to communication among Dominicans.

The original Indian languages are no longer spoken in the country, but some Indian words and names still survive. (A contemporary political leader, for example, is named after the Indian chieftain Caonabo.) None of the African dialects are of any importance today either. In language as in culture, Indian and African patterns gave way to European ones.

Other languages are occasionally heard. The Chinese and Japanese may speak their native languages among themselves. In cane-growing areas and along the frontier, Haitian French or *patois* may be spoken. English may also be heard occasionally

in the capital, on the Samaná Peninsula, or in areas where immigrants from the former British colonies in the Caribbean have
settled; but English is not the "second language" of the Dominicans as it is for, say, the nearby Puerto Ricans. Generally,
Dominicans tend to resent the use in their presence of a foreign
language that they cannot understand.

Standard spoken Spanish is given added emphasis by a wide
variety of hand and nose signs. These signs are employed constantly in conversation and make it appear as though the Dominican manner of speech were highly animated and emotional.
Frequently, a sign alone—without words—is sufficient to convey a great deal of meaning.

Few dialects are spoken in the Dominican Republic. Various
regions have nuances of meaning and intonation that are dis-
tinguishable to Dominicans or to the trained observer, but the
differences are not great, and a Dominican from one region
would ordinarily have no trouble communicating with one from
another. The most distinctive of the dialects is Cibaeña, which
is spoken primarily by rural, lower-class people in the northern
part of the country. Here the words may be slurred together,
their endings dropped, and a slightly more pronounced nasal
sound added. (The word *colorado* ["red"] would be pronounced
in Cibaeña as *colorão*.)

The closeness of the United States and the degree of its influence in recent years have led to the introduction of various
English words into everyday speech. Some of these words such as
"bar" and "leader" (*líder*) have been adopted because they gained
international currency or because there was no exact Spanish
equivalent. Other English words have been taken over even
though there are good Spanish equivalents, and these are less
acceptable to language purists—"sandwich," "basquetbol,"
"beisbol," "whiskey," and many more. Dominican nationalists
sometimes resent this "coca-colaization" of their language, but
to no avail. Among the legacies of two U.S. occupations of the

country in this century is the incorporation of more English words and expressions into the language. More and more Dominicans, furthermore, now study, travel, visit, or do business in the United States instead of in Europe; and English is becoming the first foreign language learned by both the educated and the uneducated. Many Dominicans of humble origins who are hardly able to write Spanish take correspondence courses in English in order to increase their job potential.

As in most Latin American countries, the command of language generally distinguishes the educated from the uneducated. Training in oratory and rhetoric is considered essential in education; and the successful man, particularly in politics, usually has superior ability in the spoken word and in declamation. Indeed, good oratory is often more persuasive than rational argument, and those who can, with flourish and imagery, skillfully manipulate words are widely admired. It is probably no accident that a writer like Bosch, who had a wonderful way with words but who was less able as an administrator, could, as he did in 1962, win the presidency in a landslide.

RELIGIONS

The Dominican Republic has, since the establishment of Spanish rule, been a Roman Catholic country: current statistics tell us that 98.2 per cent of the population is Catholic, 1.4 per cent Protestant, and 0.4 per cent "other." The Protestants include Baptists, Methodists, Presbyterians, Jehovah's Witnesses, and others, all of whom the Dominicans tend to lump together as *Evangélicos*. The "others" include Jews, spiritualists, Muslims, and Buddhists.

Although Catholicism has traditionally been the official state religion, religious freedom exists. And though the country is overwhelmingly Catholic, religion does not seem to be as strong a force in the Dominican Republic as it is in some other Latin

American countries. Most Dominican men, though at least nominally Catholic, feel that religion is more a matter for women and children. While their families attend church, the men may be playing dominoes or watching a cock fight. In many homes, pictures of the Virgin of Altagracia (the national patron saint) may hang side by side with family pictures and skimpily clad calendar girls. In contrast to the official statistics, most estimates are that only 10 per cent of the population are active, practicing Catholics.

The Church itself is organized as follows: at the top of the hierarchy is the Archbishop of Santo Domingo; beneath him are four bishops who exercise jurisdiction over their respective regions. In 1963, there were only 390 priests in the entire country, that is, one priest for every 7,800 Catholics. While understaffed —even by Latin American standards—the Church maintains considerable influence over the moral and spiritual, as well as the political and social, life of many Dominicans.

The Church in the Dominican Republic is not a large landowner. It has no *latifundia* or industrial wealth, and therefore it cannot back its pronouncements with economic force. The Church's influence is thus limited to the moral suasion of its statements. This suasion matters a great deal to some Dominicans, but the Church is not strong enough so that its stand on political questions is often decisive. In alliance with other sectors of the population, however, its weight can tip the balance.

It is necessary to make these statements because the Dominican Church, like the Church in the rest of the world, has been caught up in the contemporary revolution involving the attempt of underdeveloped countries to bridge the transition to modernity. While the Church would like to benefit from a close alliance with the modernizing elements, it nevertheless hesitates to alienate and cut itself off from those who stand for the traditional *status quo*. This conflict has severely rocked and split the Church and its flock in the Dominican Republic.

Historically, the Dominican Church has never been overly powerful. Most priests went to the more populous and wealthier areas of Latin America. Perhaps because the Church has always been relatively weak, the Dominican Republic, unlike Mexico, for example, has not had a history of violent anticlericalism. Nevertheless, the Church was long identified with the land-owning elite, the traditional holders of power in the country.

During the Trujillo dictatorship, Church and state continued to work closely together. The Church under Archbishop Pittini and the dictatorship under Trujillo mutually aided and benefited each other and jointly reaped the short-term rewards of their close association. It was only during the last two years of his rule that the Church began to criticize Trujillo's dictatorship.

After Trujillo's assassination, the Church adopted an increasingly liberal stand on many important issues. It urged an end to injustice and tyranny and called for agrarian reform, free elections, social justice for the lower classes, and a more democratic system. Not all of the clergy shared these sentiments, but most saw the need for sweeping reforms and felt that the Church should begin to identify more with the "revolution of rising expectations."

While the Church was theoretically in favor of increased democracy, it did not favor the form that democracy took under Bosch. Even before the 1962 elections, some priests were calling Bosch a "Marxist-Leninist," and the presidential candidate of the PRD and his most outspoken accuser then locked horns in a celebrated television debate. Significantly, Bosch was at that time able to take political advantage of the Church's opposition. But the attacks of the Church continued after his inauguration.

The PRD was criticized for promulgating a "godless" constitution, and a series of "Christian anti-Communist" crusades rallied certain conservative sectors of the population against the government. There is little doubt that the Church's opposition to Bosch, as well as the vitriolic cries of certain priests who thought the President might be a second Castro, contributed significantly to the overthrow of the Bosch administration.

The Church was subsequently discredited with many Dominicans for its role in the overthrow of the constitutional government, but this antagonism remained latent until the 1965 revolution revealed the full depths of anti-Church sentiment in the Dominican Republic. Many Constitutionalists identified the Church with the oligarchy and the military as being responsible for the ills that plagued the country. Since the 1965 upheaval, however, the Church has made extensive efforts to identify itself with the advocates of social change, with the doctrines expressed in the papal encyclicals *Rerum Novarum*, *Quadragesimo Anno*, and *Mater et Magistra*, and with the reform movement begun by Pope John XXIII. It is still too early, however, to say whether these efforts will enable the Church to regain its lost prestige.

The Dominican Republic's attempt to bridge the transition from a traditional, semi-feudal society to a more modern nation produced severe divisions within the Church. The division remains primarily between those clerics who hark back to the peace and order of the traditional society and those who see the traditional order as an anachronism and who thus want to side with reform and social change. These divisions have split the Church along several different lines. On the one hand, of the 390 priests in the country, only 50 (or 14 per cent) are native-born; and many Dominicans believe that the remaining large foreign majority of 340 does not always have the best interests of the Dominican Republic at heart. The younger priests, furthermore, tend to be more liberal and more interested in reform than their very conservative superiors. The various clerical orders working in the country—of which the Jesuits are the largest, the most militantly anti-Communist, and the most controversial —are often in disagreement. Also, the papal nuncio, the representative of the Vatican in Santo Domingo, at times works at cross purposes with the country's archbishop and bishops.

Catholicism, it goes without saying, remains the overwhelmingly dominant religion in the country. Although many towns have local holy men, seers, and medicine men (or women), and though rather strange mixtures of Catholic and African cults are practiced along the Haitian frontier, the Roman Catholic faith is shared, at least nominally, by almost all Dominicans. To be a Dominican, indeed, is to be Catholic. But though they share this common faith, Dominicans—and the Church itself—are severely divided on basic social and political questions which the Church feels fall within the province of its moral leadership. This theme—severe division and fragmentation, despite apparent uniformity—will be encountered many times again in analyzing other aspects of the Dominican system.

VALUES AND BEHAVIOR

There is probably no such thing as a Dominican national character. Individual Dominicans obviously have different outlooks and perspectives, and they cannot be neatly type-cast according to this or that trait. Nevertheless, many Dominicans seem to share certain values and beliefs that influence their behavior and distinguish them from the peoples of other cultures.

Like other Latin Americans, Dominicans value highly the dignity of the individual. Personal integrity is more important than abstract rights or institutions, and personal honor and dignity tend to take priority over group responsibility. In political terms this means that loyalty goes more to the person than to the party or government he may head. The emphasis upon the dignity of the individual and the social and political values arising from it have been called *personalismo*.

Personalism tends to make grand heroic deeds more important than day-to-day chores. It also helps give rise to *machismo*, that is, emphasis on "maleness." The all-conquering hero, the man on horseback, the lady-killer, the bullfighter, the flamboyant and dominating personality who sees his world not just as a stage but as a stage on which he must act dramatically, heroically, with good humor, and a sense of fatalism—this is the kind of man whom Dominicans tend to admire. The colorless bureaucrat, the paper-shuffler, the efficient but undramatic administrator is little respected.

Machismo may also be displayed by success in athletics, intellectual exploits, or guerrilla activity. Juan Bosch's hesitancy to return to the Dominican Republic from his exile in Puerto Rico during the height of the shooting in the 1965 revolution and his refusal to leave his house during the 1966 election campaign for fear that he might be assassinated demonstrated to Dominicans a lack of *machismo*, and it undoubtedly contributed to his electoral defeat. An individual should additionally possess a sense of irony and wit and should be able to display his abilities in a distinctive, dramatic fashion. Death for a glorious cause may also be looked upon as a means to achieve one's personal destiny.

Even within the family, the cult of the male is the rule. Women occupy an inferior position and are expected to supervise and take care of the children and the home. To a degree, however, the traditional family structure is beginning to break down. Some women have achieved professional status and others, young girls especially, are now finding jobs as typists and secretaries. Many Dominican men, on the other hand, have two families or assert their affluence and their *machismo* by maintaining a mistress. A sizable proportion simply leave their families to fend for themselves. Dominican family ties, particularly among the lower classes, are probably weaker and more unstable than in most Latin American countries; and the family as an institution has only a precarious existence.

And yet, familial considerations are still most important in social relations. The *compadrazgo*, for example, links the godfather not only with his godson but also with the godson's family. It is the norm for a government official to favor relatives and his *compadrazgo*-linked intimate friends over strangers. Nepotism is frequently the expected mode of behavior. Family ties, together with the personal trust and confidence that go with them, are more important than impersonal ability.

Idealism is also an important part of the Dominican character. While the ordinary and the mundane are deprecated, the utopian ideal—usually extreme, absolute, and unattainable—is glorified. The pragmatic compromise, the workable solution, the idea of "getting it done" are not as highly valued in Dominican society as they are in the Anglo-American culture. Instead, compromise often is considered a personal affront to one's dignity and individualism and casts doubt upon the "rightness" of one's ideals. Consensus—a basic agreement on the ends and means of activity—would not often be possible in this context.

Individualism in the Dominican Republic is probably even more pronounced than in other Latin American countries. Dominicans do not stand in orderly lines at the theater or in grocery stores, and a meeting that does not turn into a chaotic shouting match is a rarity. Dominicans react against organization and systematization of any kind, and the result frequently is disorder and inefficiency. The Peace Corps has attempted to teach the Dominicans what it calls "organizational literacy"— that is, the minimum requirements for holding a meeting or running any kind of cooperative enterprise—but the volunteers have had little success so far. North American ideas of order and efficiency do not always jibe with Dominican conceptions of unbridled individualism.

The issues of greatest personal concern to most Dominicans are the improvement of their living standards, housing, landownership, employment, public health, and opportunities for their children. Questions related to nationalism, political stability, efficient government, Communism, and the United States have recently gained in importance but remain secondary. Dominicans consider the need for better standards of living as a national political problem to be accomplished by the government —or else. Recent surveys have shown that this demand for more food, better housing and education, etc., is a potentially greater revolutionary force in the Dominican Republic than in the other Latin American republics.

Most Dominicans feel that they are badly off in absolute terms, and they have little sense of personal improvement from year to year. They maintain some hope for the future, but their frustration, caused by misery and hunger, is extremely high. A research team hired to study the attitudes, hopes, and fears of the Dominican people came to the conclusion that "an extremely serious situation of popular discontent and frustration, fraught with a dangerous potential for upheaval, exists."[*]

Yet, the Dominicans by and large do not have the kind of ambitious, innovational, risk-taking personalities found in other cultures; and, to the frustration of some U.S. foreign-aid officials, do not always seem willing to do much to change or improve their lot. Rural peasants on the verge of starvation, however, may reason—with some justification—that while things are bad now, a change might only make them worse. Others trust that their life depends on destiny, and hoping that destiny shows its favors they buy lottery tickets week after week or wager constantly on the outcome of almost any event. Some find consolation in a kind of spiritual determinism or resignation ("si Dios quiere"—"if God wills"), and many gloomily blame their misfortune on a Dominican national malaise (somos malos—"We are bad"). There exists a kind of national inferi-

---

[*] Lloyd A. Free, Attitudes, Hopes and Fears of the Dominican People (Princeton, New Jersey: Institute for International Social Research, 1965), p. 16.

ority complex among the Dominicans; they seem to have lost faith in themselves and in their own ability to solve national problems, often preferring to "let the North Americans do it."

Dominicans tend to look with favor on democracy. They admire the United States and Venezuela and disapprove of Communism, the Soviet Union, and Fidel Castro. The landing of U.S. troops on Dominican soil sharply diminished pro-American feelings and, particularly among strongly nationalistic elements, led to intense anti-Americanism. Though they often refer to Americans as "cold," the Dominicans idolized President Kennedy and often imitate American fashions, music, comics, and TV.

The type of democratic society that the Dominicans want for themselves, however, emphasizes persons and ideals. In practice, nevertheless, a hierarchical society, in which those with leadership qualities play the role of *patrón*, is commonly accepted. Not only is the *patrón* the leader, he must also be a kind, fair, and demanding teacher and father. He grants favors (often to relatives) and expects to receive loyalty and service in return. These relations are guaranteed more by personal trust, affection, and family ties than by law. Demagogues and dictators, such as Trujillo, may see themselves as a kind of national *patrón*.

The *patrón* system prevails not only in the family but in political parties and interest associations as well. Most Dominican political parties are personalistic—that is, allegiance is given to the *líder* or *caudillo* rather than to a party program or ideology. Professional associations and labor organizations also depend on the maintenance of common loyalty and often can only be held together by impassioned personal appeals rather than the bonds of mutual interests. Impersonal and faceless groups are nearly impossible to organize in the Dominican Republic.

In this setting, compromise, governmental stability, loyal opposition, and peaceful change-over of leadership become difficult. As in 1962, electoral defeat is interpreted as a personal affront and not just as a rejection of a party program. The defeated party sees its function as that of subverting the party in power rather than in functioning as a critical but loyal opposition. By the same token, it is usually assumed that the victorious party will use its control of the government for material advantages. Since truth and righteousness are often considered absolute and one-sided, competition cannot be permitted; opposition must be considered wholly false and unrighteous. Similarly, anyone who changes his views or cooperates with the opposition is a defector and traitor.

Political appeals are thus made to universal moral principles —to democracy, human rights, constitutionalism, and the like. The lower classes are easily drawn to a messianic reformer— such as Bosch; while the upper class often advocates a return to the peace, order, and stability of a bygone era. In any case, the government is often identified with the name of its *líder*— Juan Bo', "Donny" Reid, Balaguer. Immediate satisfaction rather than long-term results is demanded. At the same time, popular local initiative has no strong tradition; instead, reliance is placed on the all-powerful "they" of the government who are responsible not just for political decisions but for the well-being of the society and of its individual members.

Dominicans also seem to have developed what might be termed a "psychology of conspiracy." This is probably a legacy of the Trujillo era, when almost all relationships were in fact conspiratorial. Dominicans hesitate to trust an impersonal authority, and they believe—historically, with good reason—that power leads inevitably to the abuse and corruption of power. Dominicans simply cannot conceive of a government that works for the good of the people and not for its own interests. To most Dominicans, honest government is thus a contradiction in terms.

In this context, the building of a democratic society—at least on the British or U. S. model—would thus be most difficult. Few of the commonly accepted ingredients of democracy—respect for elections, loyal opposition, spirit of compromise and conciliation, mutual trust, government by law and by constitution rather than by men, acceptance of the "rules of the game," governmental honesty and responsibility—are present. It may therefore be easier to understand why the country has vacillated between periods of extreme tyranny and extreme instability. Though all Dominicans clearly do not share all the characteristics we have ascribed to them, there does seem to be a special Dominican political culture which is different from those of other countries.

Above and beyond all this, the Dominicans are an exceedingly friendly and polite people. This perhaps reflects the fact that the country remains more a traditional than a mass society, where friendly personal relations are still highly valued. The revolution and civil war of 1965, however, bitterly divided many families and caused hatred and estrangement among people who had previously been close. Still, the pleasantness of the land and of the Dominican people could not disappear overnight. As Robert Crassweller has concluded, "[The Dominicans] are people of simple sweetness and good will, gentle, and casually dignified."*

These personal traits which we have considered are often contradictory—for example, the emphasis on extreme individualism and absolute liberty (verging on anarchy) versus the stress on the peace and order of an authoritarian, hierarchical structure. Furthermore, friendliness and the uniformity and relative homogeneity which exist in race, religion, language, values, and behavior do not, as we have seen, lead to an integrated society. Most Dominicans are currently torn between opposing values,

* *Trujillo: The Life and Times of a Caribbean Dictator* (New York: Macmillan, 1966), p. 12.

and in this transitional period through which the country is going they tend to be uncertain and insecure. The tendency to see issues in extreme and absolutist terms makes conflicts even more severe. Overall, however, the Dominican Republic's people still seem to be much more individually or privately focused than group- or community-centered, and this works to prevent the establishment of a unified nation.

Chapter VII

THE SOCIAL STRUCTURE

AS WE HAVE SEEN, the Dominican Republic throughout its history has been a two-class society, with a small well-to-do group, large numbers of the very poor, and only a small middle sector. The distinction between the rich, the middle groups, and the poor is not determined exclusively by wealth, however, but also involves differences of education, manners, social standing, family history, and color. The gaps between these societal sectors are thus not only large but all-encompassing, involving nearly every aspect of existence. The Dominican social structure, with its severe divisions between classes and enormous differences in life-styles and living standards, has further served to prevent the development of a united, integrated nation.

THE POOR

The Dominican Republic's poorest elements are fantastically poor by U.S. standards and considerably less well off than most of their Latin American counterparts. Though it is impossible to compute exactly, most estimates put the per capita income somewhere between $180 and $230 per year. Even this figure does not accurately indicate the extent of the poverty, for it represents only a gross average and tells us nothing about how income is distributed. In fact, the high income of relatively few Dominicans raises the average even to this low level; most people have hardly any income to speak of at all and exist, indeed, almost completely outside the money economy.

The Dominican Republic's poor live in both the cities and the countryside, the majority in the latter. Lured by rumors of jobs and a better life, many peasants have migrated to the cities in recent decades; but since the labor market is glutted and jobs are scarce, this has usually resulted only in the transfer of rural slums to the city. Urbanization of the population does not necessarily imply improved standards of living.

The *campesino* (peasant) has historically been the forgotten man in Dominican life. He has remained almost completely outside national affairs and has had no say in deciding matters that affect him most closely. The peasants produce little, consume little, and continue to live in the manner to which they have always been accustomed.

Official figures state that about six out of every ten Dominicans cannot read or write. In the countryside, however, since there are few schools and few teachers, illiteracy may run as high as 80–90 per cent.

Employment in the *campo* is difficult to find. Of the 65 per cent of the population who, in one way or another, eke out a meager existence in agriculture, only about one in five holds a job. And much of this employment is only seasonal work on the large plantations; the few *campesinos* who are fortunate enough to find jobs planting or harvesting the crops may thus work only two months of the year. More than half of the entire population can find no employment at all and must try to get by at the subsistence level. Starvation, disease, and misery afflict not a few but the majority of Dominicans.

In the United States and the countries touching on the Caribbean, there has long been a widespread belief, fostered in part by Trujillo's propaganda, that the Dominicans are well off. There is little truth in this assertion. Many of its people live little or no better than the Haitians next door, proverbially cited as the poorest and most miserable people of the hemisphere. The Dominican Republic's subsistence peasants are by far the worst off, but even the employed work only for a pittance. In the area around Cotúi, for example, cane-cutters were earning 55 cents per ton in 1962, with an entire family, including the children, able to cut only about two tons per day. And one must remember to juxtapose these figures with the prices for rice and beans—the staples of the Dominicans' diet—which are higher by far than in the United States.

Conditions of life for the *campesino* are miserable throughout the nation, but in some areas they are particularly wretched. In the rolling plains of the east, some of the large companies have put up a few low-cost housing projects, and though without water or light, these shacks are considerably better than most. In the north—the Vega Real and the Cibao—the wealth of the land and the *noblesse oblige* attitude of some of the land-owners are reflected in the relatively prosperous living conditions of the peasants. Some of the *campesinos* in this area may have store-bought clothes (however ragged) and shoes (however full of holes). Some of their houses may be made of wood, and a few may even have a floor. These peasants may own a chicken and have enough land to grow a few beans and some yucca for home consumption.

These relatively prosperous conditions are more the exception than the rule. Throughout the country, once one leaves the main highways or looks behind the model developments, the people live in extremely primitive conditions. Almost all have inadequate food, clothes, and housing; no electricity or readily available water; and no educational, recreational, or medical facilities. The rural population is widely scattered in most areas, and roads connecting the villages are not developed. Isolation from friends, relatives, the social centers, and markets adds to the people's misery.

The better huts (*bohíos*) are built of palm planking with palm or banana-leaf roofs. Most are patched together with thatch, mud, old newspapers, and leaves and provide only the barest protection from rain or sun. The floor is packed earth, and the furnishings are usually limited to a few stools, a rickety chair, and a cot or two. On a picture postcard these shacks may look almost idyllic, nestled against a lush green backdrop on a clear sunny day; in reality, the life in them is hard, miserable, and usually short.

Many peasants build their *bohíos* on unused private land or on public property, as on the edge of a road. They could be evicted at any time—and often are. Most do not have enough land to raise sufficient food for their own families and are perpetually in debt to the village store. At the same time, however, some of the large estates have not been put to productive use. The twin problems of *minifundia* (a plot which is too small to be economical) and *latifundia* (unused large plots) are thus both present in the Dominican Republic.

The village is the center of social and economic life. It usually includes a church, a bar-restaurant, a single paved street (often with curbs built by Trujillo), various houses, and several *tiendas* (small stores) whose radios provide an attractive lure for the residents of the area. In many instances, the most imposing buildings in the community are the military post and Trujillo's old Partido Dominicano headquarters, now in ruins or in the process of being converted into a school or medical center.

Without medical attention, the children in the rural areas are often diseased and malformed. Since cloth is expensive, they run around naked during their early years, wallowing in the same grime and filth as the village animals. The water is polluted, and food is scarce. Many children have the bloated bellies that denote malnutrition; scars and infections cover their bodies. The moral problem of the many broken families seems insignificant compared to the practical problem—the women are usually forced to grub for clothing and for unhealthy and inadequate food for their many children.

Even the few professional people—dentists, teachers, lawyers

—in the towns that dot the countryside live in houses that most Mississippi sharecroppers could match. In Cristóbal, a community of 2,000 near the Haitian border, for example, there is no electricity or medical dispensary; the nearest possible employment—at the Barahona sugar complex—is thirty miles away and hardly feasible for those who may not even have a burro. Bathing is done in an old canal, which is four miles away and which also serves as the water supply, carried every day in large cans on the heads of the women. The difficult conditions give rise to despair. As one resident put it, "Here we have nothing—not even women. They are too busy working." The town and its problems have been ignored. The people claim that no government official has visited them in years. And Cristóbal is not unique.

Statistics do not tell a very colorful story, but the following may serve to better illustrate the conditions of life in the countryside. A recent survey of a group of rural Dominican youth revealed that three-fourths lived in houses made of mud, leaves, and sticks, with no floors and no electricity. Ninety per cent ate only rice and beans habitually, and 59 per cent came from homes where neither mother nor father could read or write. Three-fifths worked for less than 30 cents a day—when they worked. Prices in the country were higher than in the city, and credit could only be obtained at usurious interest rates. The conclusion was that the rural Dominicans' diet was inadequate, that their housing and facilities were insufficient, and that a series of vicious circles—poverty, illiteracy, lack of opportunities, starvation, low wages, debt, lack of jobs, disease—trapped them in a life from which they could not escape.*

Not only is the Dominican peasant fantastically poor, but he is also, in terms of per capita productivity, inefficient. The unmechanized, uneconomical nature of rural employment is em-

* Carlos Campos and Alberto Arredondo "Las condiciones de vida del campesino dominicano," *Panoramas*, No. 4 (July–August, 1963), 81–110.

phasized by the fact that one Dominican agricultural worker produces only enough food for five other persons, while his counterpart in an economically more advanced society may produce enough for twenty or more.

Living conditions for the peasant are so bad that the possibility of improvement is hardly considered. This is perhaps the most tragic aspect. The poverty is so great that even hope is lost. Only a sense of dignity remains.

Because the situation in the countryside is so hopeless, many *campesinos*, we have said, began to migrate to the capital city in the hope of finding permanent employment and a higher standard of living. But work in Santo Domingo, where the population doubled between 1950 and 1960, was not always available, and the displaced peasants joined the ranks of the urban unemployed. The unemployment rate mushroomed to 40 per cent. Occasionally, the newcomers to the city found temporary work as stevedores, peddlers, bottle collectors, housemaids, or prostitutes, but their existence remained tenuous.

These urban peasants have set up shacks, much like the ones they inhabited in the country, in Santo Domingo's teeming slums, especially along the Ozama River. Crowded, filthy, without water, electricity, or sanitation, filled with naked, diseased, starving children, with rats and pigs competing for the meager food—these shanty towns constructed of strips of bark and old packing cases grew much faster than the government's housing and welfare programs. Sometimes the city's poor moved into run-down mansions—such as those formerly owned by the Trujillos—and divided them into the smallest of units. With little to do and no hope left, the unemployed urban *campesino* was ripe for a demagogic appeal or for violent change. These elements flocked to the Constitutionalist side during the revolution of 1965.

The employed urban lower class, including the workers in the large sugar mills, are better organized than the peasantry and enjoy a slightly higher standard of living. Their labor unions are still in their infancy, and social legislation is not always implemented, but in the countryside, in comparison, not even the rudiments of an organizational structure exist, and welfare benefits are wholly nonexistent. In contrast to the rural *campesinos*, moreover, the urban poor generated revolutionary fervor, for they had at least the hope and expectation that a better life could be achieved.

However, urban workers and rural peasants alike remain at the bottom of the social pyramid, with few opportunities for advancement. The political parties compete for their votes, but the vote of the poor every four years counts for little beside the real power centers located elsewhere in the society. Agrarian reform programs—including not only the distribution of state-owned lands but also educational facilities, credit unions, social centers, housing, irrigation, and cooperatives—have been continually promised; but the programs are either limited in scope, do not get off the ground, or consist only of promises. Attempts to mobilize the peasantry and urban labor—to give them an organized voice and some bargaining power—are continuously frustrated. The Bosch government was dedicated to improving the lot of these traditionally forgotten and ignored poor, but it was overthrown after only seven months in office. The task of integrating the majority of the Dominican population into the national, social, economic, and political life remains to be accomplished; and the barriers against full integration are huge.

THE MIDDLE SECTORS

Since the time of Columbus, Hispaniola has had a few people who were not particularly well off but who were not impoverished either. The earliest middle groups included soldiers, artisans, craftsmen, and a few merchants; today, they come from a wider range of income and occupational groups.

The Dominican Republic's middle sectors share little beside the fact that they cannot be classified as either rich or poor. They do not have a set of values and beliefs that distinguishes them clearly from other classes, and they do not have a sense of class consciousness. They are a diverse group rather than a unified class; and it is for this reason that we refer to them as the "middle sectors" or the "middle groups" rather than the "middle class." Numerically they are small; their self-identification is practically nonexistent.

These sectors now include the soldiers, artisans, craftsmen, and merchants of the "old" middle class, as well as the professionals, small businessmen, managers and foremen, government workers, personnel in transportation and communications, salesmen and clerks, secretaries, shop-owners, and so on, of the "new" middle class. The ranks of the middle groups may also include the younger members of well-to-do families and also the economically more secure and better-educated members of the lower class. They are mostly concentrated in the cities, but a few also live in the countryside. These sectors have widely differing perspectives and interests and do not think, function, or behave as a unit.

About all that these various middle sectors can agree on is that they do not want to be considered as poor and ranked with the lower class, and that they would like to be thought of as more prosperous and prominent than is actually the case. They are socially ambitious and tend to imitate upper-class ways. A clerk working in a store may be earning less than a stevedore, but since the clerk wears a white shirt and a tie and does not do manual labor, he considers himself and is considered by others socially superior. In their eagerness to imitate upper-class living standards, members of the middle sectors may buy a car, hire a maid, or build a house and, in so doing, live far beyond their means.

In the Dominican Republic, some important economic, social,

and political differences exist between the commercial, professional, and governmental elements within the middle sectors.
The commercial segment (which contains a considerable number
of Spanish immigrants) is of course engaged in business and
hence benefits from peaceful and stable conditions that favor business. These business elements generally do not participate directly
in partisan politics but channel their pressure on the government
through a number of commercial associations. It is probably no
coincidence that Spanish businessmen led the opposition to the
Bosch government in 1963. The commercial element, extremely
insecure because its wealth and social standing is so precarious,
is even more strongly opposed to programs of social justice for
the lower classes than is the Dominican elite.

The professional component of the middle sector differs from
the commercial one chiefly in terms of its educational background. Many professionals are sons of merchants and shopkeepers who wanted a better life for their children and saved
enough money to send them to the university. Medicine, law,
engineering, and architecture seem to be the favorite professions.
In fact, there is a surplus of graduates in many professional
fields, and the country is not able to absorb or find sufficient
work for them all. Both because of their educational background
and the fact that they are often underemployed, many professionals enter politics. The executive committees of most political
parties are thus composed almost exclusively of those with a
professional background. By training and inclination, they tend
to be philosophers rather than technicians. Most are urbane,
civilized, and at home with ideas, but not with everyday routines
of running a party. The political boss, as we know him in the
United States, is virtually nonexistent in the Dominican Republic.
The government tends to become the largest employer of these
professionals. Many of them, furthermore, are far more liberal
or middle-of-the-road than are their commercial, middle-sector
counterparts. Some, especially the alienated intellectuals, em-

brace radical political ideologies; relatively few become conservative defenders of the *status quo*.

The politics of the government employees cannot be determined so easily. Many of the technicians favored Bosch in the 1966 presidential campaign, but they had not done so in 1962. Those who worked at more menial tasks—the garbagemen, electrical workers, and so forth—belonged to labor organizations controlled by the extreme left. Middle-level government employees have more ambiguous political sentiments, often preferring to remain apolitical rather than to declare their beliefs and run the risk of losing their jobs in a country that has no effective civil-service law. This group also considers government employment as its special preserve and often uses public office to further its own interests or those of family and friends.

The middle sector also includes labor leaders, who sometimes use the power of the workers they control and represent to further their own social and political ends. Mass support in the form of votes and demonstrations is sometimes provided for the middle sectors by lower-class elements. At the other end of the social spectrum, some of the elite, influenced by the university atmosphere, often join middle-sector groups in expressing radical nationalist and radical reformist programs.

The armed forces officer corps is also a preserve of the middle sectors and has enabled some members of those groups to rise to national prominence. Indeed, the armed forces are a channel of political and economic advancement for the middle *and* lower classes. Most officers come from rural, middle-sector families—the sons of merchants and storeowners. The ranks, however, are filled with poor *campesino* youths. These enlisted men receive a uniform, adequate food, quarters, salary, and a gun—which gives them a position and rank they could not otherwise obtain. An officership carries with it possibilities for enrichment and the exercise of power on a grand scale. The armed forces also perform certain educational functions and champion nationalism (often extremist) at the expense of regionalism or localism.

The middle sectors are divided horizontally as well as vertically. In Juan Bosch's analysis,* the "high middle" class, numbering some 15,000 adults (including some foreigners) and composed of the more successful businessmen, professionals, landowners, and industrialists, is secure in its wealth and social standing but is deficient in nationalism and lacks a sense of social justice. The "middle middle" class, consisting of some 150,000–200,000 adults, contains most of the professionals, government officials, and small businessmen; as a class it is very insecure and also lacks moral fiber. The "lower middle" class, numbering about 150,000, consists of merchants, clerks, and craftsmen and is also insecure. In Bosch's view, almost the entire middle sector (perhaps 10–15 per cent of the entire population) is uncertain about its future and without moral values or a sense of loyalty to the nation.

Consciousness of skin color and family background is very pronounced among the middle sectors. While the elite is clearly white and the lower classes clearly dark, the middle groups are varying degrees of mulatto. Middle-sector elements usually *consider* themselves white, however, and they are more likely than others to check closely the family history of the persons their children associate with or marry.

Many members of the middle sectors join clubs or associations. These include social clubs (*centros*); groups like the Rotary Club, Masons, or Odd Fellows; and professional or business associations. While the *centros* and neophilanthropic organizations are ordinarily not politically active, the professional associations often function as political pressure groups. One or another of them publishes daily communiqués in the Dominican press, giving its point of view on political issues. Often, professional

* *The Unfinished Experiment: Democracy in the Dominican Republic* (New York: Frederick A. Praeger, 1965).

associations are more influential in national politics than the parties are and have sometimes served as a stepping-stone to national prominence or public office for their leaders.

The Dominican middle sectors are thus not a unifying force in the society. They do not share many beliefs and have not been notable for their willingness to compromise their differences. There is no such thing as a middle-class society, with all its supposed concomitant virtues, developing in the Dominican Republic. What often goes by the name of "the middle class" is not a class at all, with common values and a sense of class consciousness, but a collection of diverse sectors, not poor and not wealthy either, which have a wide variety of outlooks, interests, and political orientations. The Dominican middle sectors are divided and fragmented, just like Dominican society as a whole.

THE ELITE

The Dominican Republic does not have a landed and noble elite that can trace its ancestry back to the Spanish conquest. Its oligarchy is of a more recent vintage, and its wealth is not nearly so great as that of most Latin American aristocracies. Also, the Dominican elite includes some of the most progressive and able people in the country.

The oligarchy is centered in the Cibao, in the city of Santiago de los Caballeros (Santiago of the Gentlemen, as it is appropriately named), but is also represented in Santo Domingo and other parts of the country. Though it constitutes no more than a very small percentage of the population (less than 100 families), its interests are extensive. Not only does the elite dictate the attitudes of society and condition its social rhythm, but it has run the Dominican Republic during most of its independent history. When two members of the oligarchy recently married, they counted no less than seven former presidents in the two family trees.

The oligarchy is interrelated by blood and marriage. The most prominent families—Cáceres, Cabral, Bermúdez, Espaillat, Taváres, Mejía—have closely interrelated histories. Other families, such as that of *Consejo* President Bonnelly, are related to the elite by marriage. Some, like the Trujillos, attempt to force acceptance by the elite, but these *nouveaux riches* are quickly rebuffed.

The elite families usually have so many connections that they are able to protect their interests no matter what direction the government in power takes. Even if one of them were not president, the odds would still be that several elite members would hold cabinet or other important government positions. Personal contact between family members or friends at the highest levels of business and government is constantly maintained. And, since they are among the best educated and the most competent people in the country, both left-of-center and right-of-center governments must rely on them for assistance.

The younger and middle-aged generations are usually the ones most involved in national affairs. The patriarch of the family, who helps to keep it together and is sometimes the ultimate arbiter of family affairs, is often not a public figure at all. Some writers think that the matriarchs, or *grandes dames*, have a great deal to say about marriages and, directly or indirectly, control much of the nation's social life.

Members of the elite are not necessarily in agreement on social or political questions. Most of the old oligarchy are moderate in their outlook and middle-of-the-road in their politics. Some of the more prominent make little secret of the fact that they voted for Bosch and the PRD; several even worked in his government. Others, however, resist any change and are apt to accuse those who push reform of being "Communists."

As to their social conscience, the oligarchs are paternalistic and humanitarian. They feel obligated to help the poor and to provide food, clothing, medicine, and sometimes money for the needy. Often, this charity is given publicly and only serves to accentuate the gap between rich and poor. On the other hand, the elite families are extremely practical and realistic. They are fully aware of the revolutionary currents sweeping Latin America and of the dire fate in neighboring Cuba for an oligarchy that refused to accept any change or reform. Members of the Dominican elite are beginning to recognize that they are likely to lose everything if they grant nothing to the aspiring poor and middle classes.

Contrary to popular notions, the oligarchy does not work closely with the armed forces. Their sons do not choose military careers, and they retain few contacts with the officer corps. They often despise the uneducated and uncouth members of the armed forces, whom the elite refer to as *"campesinos* with guns." They also regarded Trujillo and his cronies in this light and managed to retain much of their influence—or at least their dignity—despite his efforts to destroy them. Alliances of the wealthier groups with the military are based on expediency and usually do not last very long.

The elite disdains manual labor, avoids routine jobs, and generally hires others to do manual work. Domestics are employed around the house and clerks and messenger boys around the office. This is by no means to say, however, that members of the elite shun work—they work at creative decision-making levels and usually work harder than anyone around them.

The family fortunes of the oligarchy come from different sources. Rum or tobacco forms a nucleus for some of their wealth; other wealth comes from the land and from a variety of commercial or industrial enterprises. Family tradition is sometimes as important as wealth—those who are wellborn but have lost part of their fortune still regard themselves as upper class.

Though not ostentatious in the display of wealth, the upper class lives well. Their homes are not exceedingly large, but they are comfortable and very well kept, and they have all the modern conveniences. Some are now building in the suburbs, but closeness to the central squares of the cities has traditionally been a mark of high social status. Many maintain cottages at the beach or in the cool mountains and own land in the plush valleys. They may go to Puerto Rico or the United States several times a year on business or pleasure, and they frequently travel to Europe. Just as members of the middle sectors desire a university education for their children, so the members of the elite send their children abroad, now mostly to the United States.

Some upper-class elements join plush clubs, but most center their social activities around the home. Though many of them are agnostics or only nominally Catholic, the elite is often associated with the Church's position on moral, social, and political questions. This identification is bolstered because both Church and the oligarchy emphasize similar standards of respectable behavior. However, few sons of well-to-do families become priests.

What strikes one as perhaps the most interesting aspect of the Dominican oligarchy is that it is not, as is often pictured, a monolithic group steadfastly opposed to democracy and reform in any fashion. In fact, a good number are very forward-looking and concerned with development projects. There are, of course, some die-hard reactionaries in the oligarchy, but there is at least an equal number of progressives. Elite elements, like others in the society, differ on a wide range of issues; members of the elite can thus be found at all positions from left to right on the political spectrum.

MOBILITY AND SOCIAL CHANGE

Class lines in the Dominican Republic, as we have seen, are tightly drawn. Occasionally, a Dominican from one class will advance on the social scale, but he is the exceptional case. Throughout history, a Dominican of one class married someone of equivalent standing, and his children would, in turn, belong to the same class. The life cycle was repeated, generation after generation, with little change. Few channels of communication or intercourse existed between classes, and seldom could an individual move from one class to another.

Not only were the lines between the classes rigidly maintained, but the life styles were totally unrelated. While Dominicans shared a common language and the same religious, cultural, and even racial background, the classes were worlds apart in terms of dress, education, housing, influence, wealth, and sophistication. Indeed, the gaps between rich and poor were so large that they represented entirely different ways of life.

The social make-up of the Dominican Republic is changing, however, and at an accelerating pace. No longer is the country a two-class society with a few at the top controlling all the wealth and power and a large, amorphous mass at the bottom with no influence at all. As the country has begun to develop more rapidly, the social system has become increasingly complex. These social changes carry far-reaching implications for Dominican politics and for the country as a whole.

The Dominican Republic is now being profoundly affected by the impact of the world-wide industrial and technological revolution, as well as by new and revolutionary ideas about the organization of society, the economy, and the polity. The agrarian, pre-industrial, semifeudal structure is currently being challenged and severely shaken. Economic development and changing values tend to give rise to new societal sectors and organizations that not only threaten the *ancien régime* but also make the old order dependent on the new groups. The problem of accommodating new groups and new values in a traditional system that becomes more and more of an anachronism in the modern world helps to account for the instability of the present-day system.

Industrialization, for example, gave rise to an increasingly powerful labor movement. The expanding activities of the government spurred the growth of the bureaucracy; and more and more technicians, administrators, professionals, and managers were needed. The growing affluence of the entire society tended to produce more merchants, businessmen, salesmen, etc. While these processes of change are interrelated, they do not all occur at the same time. Urban groups, for example, are more quickly affected than rural groups; development has occurred unevenly.

Within the Dominican classes, then, we begin to see an increasing differentiation. The lower class now consists not only of landless peasants but also of a restless, urban proletariat. The rapidly growing middle sectors contain many commercial, professional, and other groups that disagree on a wide range of political issues and even on whether they belong to a middle class. A new business-industrial elite is rising to challenge the influence of the old landed elite.

The changes in the societal structure also increase the possibilities for social mobility. Peasants are being drawn out of the countryside into the cities. Many remain unemployed and others find jobs; in either case, living in the urban environment imparts a little more awareness of a larger world. Lower-class people may find white-collar jobs as clerks or typists, and their children may thus grow up in a middle-class environment. The military and the political parties serve as channels for upward advancement. Lower middle-class families may be able to send their children to the university; upper middle-class ones may be as talented and sophisticated as the elite. The possibilities for moving from one social class to another are increasing.

While mobility and social change are accelerating, the traditional structure, however, has proved to be durable, and class lines are by no means erased. In addition, the process of social change itself produces tensions between the newly emerging sectors. The Dominican social structure is therefore one in which not only the old class differences remain strong and thus divide and fragment the several strata, but in which divisions *within* classes have also become more pronounced. Horizontal and vertical lines chop Dominican society into a variety of sectors whose interests and points of view are still so divergent that the development of an integrated society seems at best a remote possibility.

Chapter VIII

EDUCATION AND CULTURE

DOMINICANS SOMETIMES CLAIM that theirs are the purest Spanish traditions and culture in the New World. The Dominicans have retained many of the old, formal manners of the Spanish, and their art, literature, educational system, even their *fiestas* are in the tradition of Spain. Strong efforts have been made to preserve the purity of this Spanish heritage.

The attempt to maintain the dominance of Spanish culture reflects the lack of a strong indigenous culture. There are relatively few traditions or cultural features that can be considered uniquely Dominican. Further, the purity of Spanish culture in the country has for some time been more of an ideal than a reality. Dominican customs, art, sports, and education are in fact complex mixtures of several influences. There are few native aspects which serve to strongly differentiate the Dominican Republic from other Latin American countries.

EDUCATION

A literate, educated, and technically skilled population is generally considered to be a major prerequisite for a modern and democratic system. Yet, it is only in the past five years that the Dominican Republic has begun to pay serious attention to education and to enact some fundamental educational reforms.

The idea of universal public education was foreign to the country until very recently. Education was reserved to the small elite, who had their children educated privately or sent to schools abroad. Schools existed in the larger towns for those not wealthy enough to go abroad, but in the rural areas educational facilities were practically nonexistent. Educational reform began in the late nineteenth century, however, ushered in by the great educator Eugenio María Hostos, who urged the broadening of educational opportunities and the replacement of the old system based on learning by rote with newer, more scientific pedagogical methods. But educational reform occurred slowly and almost imperceptibly; and still today, over half the population is illiterate and the outmoded system of rote learning persists.

During the long Trujillo era, the progressive ideas of Hostos were shelved, and education and the educational system were employed as instruments of the dictator's control. The nation's schools were looked upon as a means for further indoctrination in the cult of the Generalissimo. Although Trujillo instigated a compaign to combat illiteracy, education was used to teach the glories of the Trujillo era from books written by his admirers. An entire generation was thus brought up which was too young to have known anything but life under Trujillo, educated for subservience to him, indoctrinated by years of extolling his virtues, and untrained in democratic rights and responsibilities.

Trujillo did not spend much time or money on education, and the entire educational system was therefore never greatly expanded. The percentage of the total budget that Trujillo devoted to education in the Dominican Republic was the lowest in Latin America. In spite of the dictator's claim to have significantly reduced illiteracy, the Pan American Union estimated that six out of ten Dominicans could not read or write. Few teachers were trained, and all the schools lacked the barest essentials—books, paper, pencils, maps, blackboards. Though Trujillo constructed a new campus for it, the University of Santo Domingo (the oldest in the hemisphere) was permitted to run down and was largely an empty façade. Lacking in faculty or facilities, its graduates often needed years of tutoring before they could be admitted to post-graduate programs abroad.

Following Trujillo's assassination, an effort to improve the educational system was begun. Because of the all-pervasive nature of Trujillo's dictatorship, educational reform had to be effected from top to bottom of the educational structure. While improvements have been started, the difficulties involved in this process are still enormous.

Illiteracy remains a major problem. The illiteracy rate of 60 per cent from the Trujillo era has been somewhat reduced in recent years—especially in the cities—but in the countryside, the proportion of those who can neither read nor write even the simplest phrases may be as high as eight or nine out of every ten. Raising the literacy level is a difficult and long-term process: in 1920, the number of children enrolled in school constituted less than 10 per cent of the school-age population; by 1964, the figure had risen to only 16 per cent.

Illiteracy encompasses the lack of training in basic skills as well as the minimal ability to read and write. The Dominican Republic is not only short of high-level technicians and managers but also of skilled workers in almost all occupational areas —craftsmen, machinists, secretaries, tradesmen, clerks. Education must hence be directed toward training for practical skills and vocations; "pure knowledge" and increased literacy rates are, in themselves, not enough.

One aspect of the twin dilemmas of illiteracy and an untrained and unskilled population remains the lack of educational facilities. In recent years, the United States, through the Alliance for Progress, has begun to tackle this problem by helping to build schools, but these construction projects have been few in number and mostly in the cities. Writing materials and other classroom equipment are still scarce, with the result that many of the outwardly impressive new schools are little more than hollow shells.

Another factor is the lack of trained and competent teachers. In 1964, there were only 12,000 teachers for 540,000 school children in the entire country—or one teacher for every forty-five students. A disproportionately large number of teachers was concentrated in urban areas, and it was estimated that some 300,000 Dominican children—mostly rural—went without any education because of the teacher shortage. What may be even more disturbing is that almost half of the teachers had no more than the equivalent of a junior high school education. Furthermore, the highly politicized National Teachers' Federation (FENAMA) was dominated by the extreme left and frequently proved to be a very disruptive element.

The Dominican Republic does not have sufficient funds to effect sweeping reforms in its educational system. In 1963, for example, the total budget of the country amounted to some $160 million, of which $16 million was devoted to education. Though the 10 per cent of the budget reserved for education in 1963 was about double what it had been during the Trujillo era, $16 million does not carry education very far. In the more developed countries, a small college with 5,000 students may easily have an annual budget of $16 million; in the Dominican Republic, however, this sum had to cover the entire educational system, and it was simply inadequate.

Insufficient funds, shortage of teachers, and lack of facilities are related in a series of interlocking vicious circles. A teacher's salary, for example, ranges from $60 to $150 *per month*, and at this low wage, it is difficult to attract better people to teaching. U.S. assistance, while considerable, has not been sufficient to break the pattern. The opportunities for Dominican youths to improve their lot through education are thus extremely limited.

The better schools in the country are privately run, but these, too, are lacking in facilities and resources. The Catholic Church operates a number of schools, most of which are better equipped and have better teachers than the public institutions. Children of U.S. officials and of other foreign residents as well as some Dominican children attend the American (Carol Morgan) School, which is probably the nation's best.

Few technical schools have as yet been established. The liberal professions of medicine, philosophy, and the law were traditionally the most popular, and only recently has it become possible to study other technical or practical professions—engineering, architecture, or social work. The possibility of acquiring a vocational education has also been extremely limited, but now schools for secretaries, mechanics, stenographers, and clerks have begun to spring up. The recently founded agricultural institute in Santiago is also a significant step forward in vocational-technical education. These changes, however, still affect only a very small number of Dominicans.

Political instability in the post-Trujillo years has further served to restrict the possibilities for educational reform. The only Dominican government during this period that was genuinely interested in improving education on a grand scale was Bosch's. Bosch envisioned a mammoth adult-education program not only to reduce illiteracy but also to train the Dominicans in the many technical skills that the country so sorely needed. Materials were printed, teachers (including Peace Corps members) were recruited, and educational television programs were prepared. But before this ambitious and forward-looking mass literacy and training drive got off the ground, the Bosch government was overthrown, and the whole project collapsed. Subsequent Dominican governments have not attempted educational programs on such a grand scale.

What has been said so far applies chiefly to primary and secondary education, but similar problems are found at the high-school (*colegio*) and university levels. During the Trujillo era, a new physical plant was built for the national university, and several new *colegios* were constructed; but the students could not organize or engage in political activity, the professors had no security, academic freedom did not exist, books and laboratories were poorly provided for, and little in the way of practical or technical studies were taught.

Shortly after Trujillo's assassination, the Federation of Dominican Students (FED) was founded. This federation, which included both high-school and university students, seemed to be more interested in political than educational reform, and the schools soon became centers of highly partisan—and frequently violent—political activities. Through the federation, the students won autonomy for the university, succeeded in removing *trujillista* professors and rectors, and participated in numerous strikes, demonstrations, parades, and rallies. Political activity and political considerations, however, precluded the improvement of education itself. For example, the students refused to accept a university reform that would have initiated entrance examinations to weed out the unqualified because this was considered "undemocratic."

Almost all of the activist students became revolutionary leftists and radical nationalists, some, of course, more radical and revolutionary than others. The dominant student group was the intensely nationalistic, anti-imperialistic and pro-Castro Fragua (literally, "Forge"). Fragua's closest competitor was a Social Christian group, which, as many Dominicans like to point out, was far less Christian than it was Marxist. The most moderate student organization—also the smallest—was aligned with Bosch's PRD. Though most of the activist students were sympathetic to Castro's revolution and critical of the United States, they were also chauvinistically patriotic. Few became outright Communists, although the causes which the students espoused often coincided with those the various Communist groups advocated.

Although the Autonomous University of Santo Domingo is still the largest and most important, two other universities have been founded in the post-Trujillo period. These are the Catholic University Madre y Maestra, established in Santiago by the Conference of Dominican Bishops with the backing of business leaders from the local elite as well as the Ford Foundation and others, and the Pedro Henríquez Ureña National University in Santo Domingo. The founding of two new universities, in turn, has given new impetus to the entire university-reform movement.

A sharp division exists between generations in the Dominican Republic: between those of the older generation who cooperated with or acquiesced in Trujillo's regime and those of the younger generation who have grown to maturity since that time. The younger generation, frequently led by the students, rejects many of the values and traditions of the older generation; and the revolution of 1965 served as their rallying cry. While relatively few are activists, almost all tend to be revolutionary, anti-military, pro-democratic, nationalistic, and anti-imperialist (usually meaning anti-U.S.). This generation will dominate the country in the coming decade; and although some of the youths will doubtless lose the intensity of their revolutionary fervor as they grow older, the implications of their coming dominance are enormous—both for the Dominican Republic and for the United States.

CULTURE

It is often difficult, we have stated, to determine a distinctly Dominican culture. Unlike Mexico—or even Haiti—for example, there are few aspects of Dominican art, literature, or traditions that can easily be identified as purely Dominican. Indeed, the absence of a unique cultural tradition has led to the borrowing or imitating of foreign themes and to the mixing of outside influences with the dominant Spanish culture. The lack of an unadulterated and genuinely Dominican cultural tradition has also served to retard the growth of self-identity, patriotic pride, and national unity.

Literature and the Arts

Santo Domingo, the "cradle of America," was the first area of the New World to receive the imprint of European culture. During the first fifty years of Spanish rule, the island shared some of the splendor of the Spanish courts of Ferdinand and Isabella, Charles V, and Philip II; and it was from here that many of the projects and plans to explore, conquer, settle, and evangelize the Americas were launched. Santo Domingo had the first schools, convents, and university in the hemisphere, and it remains proud of this noble, albeit remote, Spanish past.

As the colony first prospered and later decayed, so its art and literature rose and declined. From the beginning, literature, the theater, and other arts flourished. Among the most prominent literary figures were Fr. Las Casas, the defender of the Indians; Oviedo, the historian of the conquest; Tirso de Molina and Bernardo de Valbuena, two of the great poets of Spain's "Golden Century"; the great preacher Fr. Alonso de Cabrera; and writers of high quality such as Archbishop Carvajal, Eugenio de Salazar, and Alonso de Zorita. The architecture—churches, monasteries, the Alcazar of Columbus, and the old city wall—was also notable. But, by the middle of the sixteenth century, most of the prominent figures had left Santo Domingo, and its flourishing culture soon declined, never fully to recover.

As the colony was neglected and became poorer, the quality and quantity of artistic and literary work also lessened. A few individuals nevertheless stood out: Juan de Castellanos, who wrote an account of the early years of Hispaniola; Antonio Sánchez Valverde, who wrote about science; Bishop Pedro A. Morell de Santa Cruz, a historian; Antonio Meléndez Bazán, a legal scholar; and Manuel de la Cruz, in the area of *belles lettres*. Intellectual life centered around the Church and the *audiencia*.

But there were not many outstanding literary figures, and few works comparable in quality to those written elsewhere in the Americas were produced. The colony was so poor, neglected, and isolated that it did not experience the literary movements and styles—baroque, rococo, and neoclassic—through which the other Spanish colonies passed. Even the eighteenth-century Enlightenment failed to revive Santo Domingo's art and literature significantly; and the island produced no literary "precursors of independence."

The succession of Haitian invasions and occupations that began in the early nineteenth century resulted in the exile of most of the colony's writers and artists. Spanish rule was reestablished during the second decade of the nineteenth century, and many of the exiles returned, but sentiment in favor of independence from the mother country grew. Among the earliest patriotic writings, those of José Nuñez de Cáceres, the leader of the movement that resulted in independence from Spain, in 1821, stand out. But another period of Haitian occupation, even more severe than the first, began in 1822, and again the intellectual elite was forced to take refuge abroad. Between 1822 and 1844, most European and Dominican cultural currents were snuffed out, the university was closed, and intellectual life came to a halt. However, the struggle of the *Trinitarios* for independence from the Haitians beginning in the late 1830's did serve as a major impetus for the revival of patriotic and nationalistic literature.

Even after independence had finally been achieved in 1844, the Dominican Republic remained isolated on the fringe of the continent, and its literary and artistic life lagged behind that of the other Latin American nations. Romanticism came to the country with Manuel María Valencia (1810–70); but "the Dominican poets of this generation never reached full vigor," in the words of the historian of Latin American literature Enrique Anderson Imbert.

A second generation of nineteenth-century romantics earned more distinction. Francisco Gregorio Billini described the customs and social life of the island in his novel *Baní*. Manuel Rodríguez Objío wrote of patriotic struggles, while the poets Salomé Ureña de Henríquez and José Joaquín Pérez stressed political and "civilizing" themes. Indigenist literature is best represented in Manuel de Jesús Galván's *Enriquillo*, the epic account of the last Indian *cacique* (chief) forcefully to oppose Spanish rule.

The beginning of realist modernism in literature came late to the Dominican Republic, as did the modernization of the country's social, economic, and political system. Though Fabio Fiallo and Gastón Fernando Deligne remained largely impervious to vernacular themes, they were influenced by modernist techniques. Federico García Godoy wrote of national history in a series of political novels; while César Nicolas Pensón collected the country's traditions in his *Cosas añejas* (*Old Times*). But modernism in the Dominican Republic came to fruition in the twentieth century with Tulio Manuel Cestero's *La sangre* (*The Blood*), describing the tyranny of Heureaux; with Manuel Troncoso de la Concha's *Narraciones dominicanas* (*Dominican Stories*), a collection of anecdotes and customs of national life; with Arturo Freites Roque's *Lo inexorable* (*The Immovable*), a satire of political intrigue; and with Rafael Damirón's *Del cesarismo* (*On Caesarism*), an account of the political conflicts of the post-Heureaux period.

During the long Trujillo era, literature and the arts reached a new low. All literary works had to conform with the official pronouncements, and the country's writers and artists were forced to produce works that glorified the dictator and his rule. The humanities and social sciences were ignored, and only histories lauding Trujillo were written. Fiction became an almost forgotten genre, and poetry sang the glories of Trujillo's accomplishments with tedious clichés. Awards, such as the Rafael L. Trujillo Prize, were bestowed on those who could best praise the regime and its chief; and the painters who portrayed him lavishly were paid well. Much of the art and architecture produced to suit Trujillo's wishes—mansions shaped like ships in a landscape of concrete waves, books and paintings comparing the dictator with God, and the like—can only be described as being in horrible taste.

A few men managed to achieve such international prominence that they could rise above the stifling dogmatism and dictatorial controls of the Trujillo dictatorship. These included the poets Héctor Inchaustegui Cabral and Manuel del Cabral, the historian Emilio Rodríguez Demorizi, the essayists and poets Max and Pedro Henríquez Ureña, and the novelist and short-story writer Juan Bosch. With Bosch, who lived in exile during most of the Trujillo regime, modern social-protest literature began.

Though some in every generation achieved a degree of distinction, the history of Dominican art and literature thus includes comparatively few noteworthy and internationally known figures and no literary or artistic giants. It therefore becomes a matter of great national pride for the Dominicans when contemporary artists such as Paul Giudiccelli and Guillo Pérez or the violinist Carlos Piantini achieve international recognition. Further, the Dominican Republic's most prominent artists and intellectuals are often almost wholly unknown even in their own country; and they do not often deal with national themes. Dominican art and literature have not provided the cultural cement that could help to consolidate the society.

Folk culture is similarly weak. There are songs, dances, poems, and stories from the northern Cibao and other regions sometimes passed from one generation to the next; but these are not commonly known and do not constitute a unifying undercurrent of folk tradition. Folk theater and music, such as that of René Carrasco and his group, is performed infrequently. Wood carvings, embroidery, mural paintings, pottery, and native songs are comparatively scarce. Both because the Indians on Hispaniola

were not a part of an advanced civilization, as existed, for example, in Mexico, Guatemala, or Peru, and because they were
so quickly decimated after the Spanish conquest, indigenous
Dominican culture hardly exists. It is also curious that the
African influence—so pronounced in Brazil, Cuba, Haiti, and
the other Caribbean islands, for example—has had so little cultural impact in the Dominican Republic. It was only during the
revolution of 1965 that a strong and widespread sense of pride
in being a Dominican seemed to emerge, which then also began
concomitantly to find expression in art and literature.

Leisure and Recreation

Leisure and recreation take many different forms in the Dominican Republic, and there are also few unifying threads in
this realm. Nevertheless, the beginning of a new movement
and of a new form of self-expression is apparent.

The *nueva ola* ("new wave"), as Dominicans call this emergent
movement, cannot be clearly or easily defined. In general, it
implies a rejection of the old and an attempt to find something
new, be it in music, writing, painting, or other artistic en-
deavors. It rejects the country's past (particularly the Trujillo
era) and seeks to arrive at a new, indigenous, nationalistic, pecu-
liarly Dominican form of expression. As such, it corresponds
closely to the wide generational division that exists between the
youth that has reached maturity in the post-Trujillo years and
the older population groups that were corrupted by his system.

The "new wave" is not a disciplined movement and has no
uniform and distinctive set of values or ideas. It is, rather, a
mood—hazy and imprecise. It may take the form of the spar-
kling Dominican music and chatter on Radio Guarachita, to
which the younger generation listens. It implies a rejection of
the gaudy international shows at the expensive tourist hotels
and a new admiration for the ironic wit and political satire of

such entertainers as Enriquillo Sánchez or Rafael Solano. It has also been expressed in paintings and murals that were inspired by the 1965 revolution. There is a new sense of pride, so much absent in past history, of things Dominican.

The *nueva ola* has not yet become clearly aligned with any political organization and, indeed, is not a "school" or a particular form of expression. Thus far, it is confined to the major cities and to towns, to people with at least a minimum involvement in national affairs. But the "new wave" is clearly identified with youth, with rising Dominican nationalism, and with the new sense of national self-identity, and will no doubt assume more and more of the political and social values of the rising generation.

Dominican leisure and recreation of course take many forms. Passing the time of day may be the most important: talking with friends, visiting relatives, sitting in the famous Dominican rocking chairs in front of one's house or apartment, passing a bottle of rum, exchanging stories with acquaintances and political allies while standing on El Conde Street at the end of the day, having one's shoes shined, ogling or commenting on the girls walking by, sipping coffee in the Café Sublime, listening to the radio at a popular rural *tienda*. These activities take precedence over the frantic rush, hurry, and impersonality characteristic of technologically more advanced "mass" societies.

Formal recreational facilities are scarce. Sports equipment is expensive, and most children do not have the means to engage in healthy and worth-while recreation. Older Dominicans may play dominoes, casino, *tablero*, or perhaps pool. Volleyball, soccer, and basketball are gaining in popularity, while golf and tennis remain the sports of the very few. The country has some spectacular beaches, where middle- and upper-class Dominicans and a few foreigners sometimes enjoy a swim. These beaches are still largely undeveloped as tourist attractions, and their natural attractiveness is not enhanced by the frequent presence of sharks close to shore. Gambling in the major hotels and casinos is sometimes legal, sometimes illegal, depending on the moral inclination and mood of the officials in power. Prostitution in the many nightclubs flourishes whether it is outlawed or not.

Movies are a popular form of entertainment and range from the expensive ($1.25) theaters for the elite in downtown Santo Domingo to the cheaper (25¢) shows for the poorer city-dwellers. While the expensive theaters may show U.S. or European releases, the cheaper, popular theaters usually present movies of the melodramatic, unrealistic, or escapist sort—with lots of blood, sex, violence, heroism, cruelty, and conquest served up with a soap-opera plot. Many of these are U.S.-made C and D grade movies, popular among the large lower class because they offer a measure of escape from the real world of poverty and frustration. Films from other Latin American countries, such as Mexico and Argentina, are also very popular. Recently, the United States Information Service has begun to show more educational films, particularly for the illiterate and isolated rural inhabitants.

Plays and concerts are offered infrequently. The "new wave" plays of Franklin Domínguez, such as his political satire *Se busca un hombre honesto* ("Wanted: An Honest Man"), achieved great popularity and were staged all over the country; but live theater is far from being a daily or even weekly event. At times, military bands give concerts in the Parque Independencia, and the firemen's band marches in nearly all civic and religious parades, but these also occur only irregularly. Concerts by the National Orchestra may be presented once or twice a year.

Dances and parties are favorite leisure activities. The most popular dance of the Dominican Republic is the *merengue*, though a slow *bolero* is sometimes interspersed with it. A *merengue* festival, held yearly, attracts visitors from neighboring countries. Parties and get-togethers at restaurants and bars usually involve drinking a great deal of the excellent Dominican rum—ordered by the bottle and never by the glass.

Baseball is definitely the national Dominican sport, and watching and discussing it are among the favorite national pastimes. Children begin playing at an early age with sticks and balls, often made of rags or even stones. Though few youths can afford proper equipment, Dominican players—Juan Marichal, Julián Javier, Ricardo Carty, and the three Rojas Alou brothers —have excelled in the United States' major leagues and are the best-known and most popular national heroes. The largest headline on the sports pages in the daily newspapers during the summer may read "Matty Rojas Alou Bats Three Singles," and the accompanying story will tell of his accomplishments in a game not even played in the Dominican Republic. Dominicans avidly follow the fortunes of the U.S. major-league teams on which their nationals play. A few years ago, some observers felt that Juan Marichal was so popular he could easily have won the race for the presidency.

The Dominican Republic has its own professional baseball league, which attracts the country's own stars as well as U.S. professionals. (Marichal at times irks Dominican nationalists who feel that he does not give his all in the Dominican league.) Four teams—the Estrellas Orientales of San Pedro de Macorís, the Aguilas Cibaeñas of Santiago, and the Escogido and Licey Clubs of Santo Domingo—compete for the championship. During the winter, Dominicans half humorously remark, baseball takes precedence over revolution. The spectators, perhaps appropriately called *fanáticos*, take a deep personal and sometimes fighting interest in their teams and their heroes; and the competition among the fans is often more intense than among the players. Few other activities are as important in the Dominican Republic as baseball.

Rafael Leónidas Trujillo, dictator of the Dominican Republic, 1930–61.

Wide World Photos

Former President Juan Bosch (*right*), exiled in Puerto Rico, listens to radio reports on the Dominican revolution of April, 1965. At left is Jaime Benítez, Chancellor of the University of Puerto Rico.　　　*Wide World Photos*

President Joaquín Balaguer—and the powers behind the throne. The occasion is a speech marking the Dominican Republic's 123d anniversary of independence from Haitian rule.

UPI Photo

Santo Domingo, Dominican Republic: Popular support for the "Constitutionalists" during 1965 rebellion.
UPI Telephoto

Damage done by U.S. guns in Santo Domingo during clash between Dominican rebels and the OAS peacekeeping forces, June 15–16, 1965. *UPI Photo*

American paratrooper stands guard in front of one of
Santo Domingo's teeming slums, after American intervention following the 1965 rebellion.   *UPI Photo*

Political rally in Santo Domingo prior
to general presidential election. U.S.
intervention had fanned anti-Americanism.   *Wide World Photos*

U.S. combat patrol lines up prisoners
after clearing an area in Santo Domingo of snipers.   *UPI Photo*

Columbus Palace in Santo Domingo,
built in 1510 by Christopher Columbus' son and recently restored as a
museum.   *Wide World Photos*

Goats being milked in back of an open-air market in
Santo Domingo.   *UPI Photo*

Urban poverty in the large slum section of Santo Domingo. *UPI Photo*

An urban housing project in Santo Domingo, seen side by side with traditional substandard dwelling. *UPI Photo*

Traditional and modern, contrast on streets of Santo Domingo. *UPI Photo*

Squatter's shanty with subsistence plot. La Herradura,
Santiago Province. *Gustavo Antonini*

Overgrazed, eroded upland in San José de las Matas
Municipality, Santiago Province. *Gustavo Antonini*

Town of Mao, important commercial and administrative center in Valverde Province. *Gustavo Antonini*

Barahona: Cooling a horse in the sugar-cane fields worked by Haitians and Dominicans. *UPI Photo*

Gutted ruins of village houses in Palma Sola, near the Haitian border. Government soldiers quash a backwoods religious cult.   *UPI Photo*

Hungry school children line up for daily CARE lunch in Santiago.   *UPI Photo*

Communications

Even in a country as small as the Dominican Republic, the lack of communications has traditionally been a major problem. The high mountains and the underdeveloped road system have always prevented easy communication between the various regions. Lack of radios and telephones meant that news traveled slowly—if it traveled at all—by foot or by burro.

One of the principal instruments with which Trujillo controlled the Dominican Republic was his near monopoly over the developing communications systems. Trujillo, it will be recalled, had greatly expanded and improved the national transportation and communication networks. The principal newspapers were completely subservient to his regime, however, and the radio and television stations were also owned or controlled by the Trujillo family. No independent expression, either over the air or on the printed page, was permitted.

In the post-Trujillo years, the Dominican Republic made a concerted effort to overcome this legacy. Newspaper circulation increased rapidly, and the papers' content was greatly improved. For the first time in more than thirty years, freedom of speech and press existed, and the number of radio stations and television and radio receivers mushroomed.

These developments are important because expanded communications grids are an essential ingredient in the modernization process. Trujillo's rule had been characterized by the isolation of all groups and individuals and the denial to them of the means of articulating or expressing their wants, demands, and interests. In the period after his assassination, communications played a major role in giving these previously isolated elements a new means of expression and thus helped to provide the country with new ideas and a growing sense of national unity.

It required some time following Trujillo's assassination before the Dominican press could achieve even the semblance of freedom, since it at first continued under the control of the Balaguer-Ramfis regime. The newspapers were filled with homage and praise to the dead dictator. The government later relaxed its controls somewhat and permitted the fledgling opposition groups to issue their own newspapers. *Unión Cívica* was the paper of the National Civic Union, *El 1J4* that of the Fourteenth of June Movement, and *El Democrático* that of the PRD. The restrictions on communications remained, however, and it was not until the rest of the Trujillo family left the country in November, 1961, that the press began to flower.

The paper with the largest circulation in Santo Domingo is *El Caribe*, owned and edited by Germán Ornes. Following the Trujillos' ouster, Ornes regained control of the paper he had lost during the dictatorship, and *El Caribe* began to urge that elections take place and that the country return to a democratic and constitutional government. Ornes used the paper as an instrument of education as well as for generally objective reporting. He fell out with the Bosch regime, and for his attacks on the government was generally discredited by the pro-Constitutionalist forces. *El Caribe*'s daily circulation of 50,000 was the highest ever reached by any Dominican newspaper.

The government-owned newspaper during most of the Trujillo era was *La Nación*. Its ownership in the post-Trujillo period was never clear, and for a time, it continued to be operated by the government at a loss. In 1963, *La Nación* closed down, only to be revived briefly by the Constitutionalists, holed up in downtown Santo Domingo during the 1965 revolution.

Replacing *La Nación* as the second newspaper of the capital city was *Listín Diario*. Though owned by an elite family, its editorials by Rafael Herrera were generally in favor of constitutionalism and increased democracy. Its features and coverage were more limited than *El Caribe*'s, and its daily circulation was about 35,000 copies.

A large number of other newspapers, magazines, and newssheets are published in the Dominican Republic. In Santiago, the daily *La Información*, with a circulation of only 7,000, provides inadequate coverage. *Prensa Libre*, a reactionary evening sheet edited by Rafael Bonilla Aybar, was for a time published in Santo Domingo. *Ahora*, the news magazine with the largest circulation, has launched a more liberal daily paper, *El Nacional*, to offset the generally conservative slant of the press. Most of the smaller towns also have newspapers that appear from time to time, but these are largely concerned with local news. For reports on national or international developments, Dominicans living outside of Santo Domingo must rely on *El Caribe*, *Listín Diario*, and *El Nacional*, which have some circulation in the countryside.

In addition, almost all groups and organizations have begun to publish their own papers. Thus, the various political parties, interest associations, student groups, and the armed forces each have their own daily, weekly, or monthly paper. The diversity of viewpoints in these papers marks a sharp change from the practices under Trujillo, when only the dictator's point of view was expressed.

Other legacies of the dictatorship in the field of communications have had to be overcome as well. The country had few trained, experienced, and capable journalists. Reporters did not know how to find, cover, or write a story. Many newsworthy events thus went unreported, facts were frequently distorted by polemic, and lively stories were often made dull. The formation of a journalists' association, of information services, and of a school of journalism at the Autonomous University represented attempts to tackle these problems. Press conferences, an unprecedented event in Dominican history, were also launched in an effort to better explain the nature and intentions of the government's programs to the people.

To fill the editorial pages, most newspapers publish writings by *pensadores*—moralists, critics, poets, philosophers, political scientists, clerics, sociologists, or publicists—who often deal with great national themes and inspiring visions. It is probably no coincidence that some of the better *pensadores*, such as Bosch, Balaguer, and Juan Isidro Jiménez-Grullón, are prominent political leaders.

The press remained generally free after the collapse of the Trujillo regime. For a time, even the Communist groups were allowed liberty of expression. Successive reports to the Inter-American Press Association have stressed the freedom the Dominican papers achieved. The press emerged as a strong enough force so that even the governments attacked and criticized by it were unwilling to interfere—unless, as in the case of Bonilla Aybar or the Communists, a sector of the press itself threatened free institutions. Given the more and better newspapers, improved coverage, greatly expanded circulation, and freedom of expression, one can say that some of the most important steps taken to erase the legacy of the fallen dictatorship occurred in the realm of the press.

The development of radio and television was in many respects similar to that of the press. During the Trujillo era, radio and television facilities were either owned by or subservient to the Trujillos, and the broadcast propaganda was similar to that in the newspapers. Some relaxation was permitted following the dictator's assassination, but it was not until the dissolution of the entire Trujillo family system that radio and television achieved a significant amount of freedom.

These media faced more problems in the post-Trujillo period than did the press. The ownership of La Voz Dominicana, Radio Caribe, Radio Rahintel, La Voz del Trópico, and others was even more confused than had been the case with *El Caribe* and *La Nación*. Inflammatory broadcasts frequently forced the government to close some radio stations. News programs usually consisted of handouts from the National Palace and brief readings of the morning's newspaper headlines. Freedom of expression was sometimes confused with a license to slander and smear.

Some degree of order, stability, and responsibility was created out of this initial chaos, and radio and television began to improve. More attention was devoted to educational and public affairs programs. Several press and publicity agencies were organized to provide newsworthy items to the stations. The ownership and directorship of stations were clarified. The statistics are even more impressive: during the time from Trujillo's last years until the mid-1960's, the number of radio stations doubled, the number of radio sets quadrupled, and the number of television sets increased ten times. Per capita ownership of radio and television sets grew until it became one of the highest in Latin America.

Radio and television also played an increasingly important role in politics. Each major party had its own radio station or time slot. Cheap and readily available Japanese transistor models enabled more and more people to listen to these programs; and in the countryside, it was not unusual to find forty or fifty individuals gathered to hear an important political broadcast. Television also became important; and some have gone so far as to attribute Bosch's 1962 electoral victory to his cleverness as a radio and television speaker. Both President Bosch and President Donald Reid Cabral pioneered in using these media to communicate directly with the population.

Despite a number of difficulties, then, developments in the press, radio, and television since the Trujillo regime was overthrown are impressive. For the most part these media play a responsible and progressive role; they seek to educate as well as to inform a public that previously showed little awareness of the conflicting ideas and intellectual currents in the outside world or even in Dominican affairs. The public information media now enjoy a freedom that never existed before. Occasionally, the newly found freedom is turned into a disservice, as in the case of those who abuse freedom of expression by calling for the overthrow of the duly constituted authority; but on the whole, the press, radio, and television have performed useful and constructive functions.

Though the public information media have improved and expanded greatly in the post-Trujillo period, the Dominican system remains, however, one in which oral communication and personal contact are at least as important as the printed or broadcast word. This is particularly true among the elite and upper middle class, who rely on their ability personally and quietly to influence their friends or relatives in business or government rather than on public communications. Family get-togethers or the telephone are thus also important in the over-all communications network. Trujillo even tried to curb these means of expression and through fear generally succeeded in shutting up the entire population. Now, however, oral communications and personal contact are again important ways of maintaining connections and gathering information.

The developments in mass communications and in interpersonal contact have contributed to the dissemination of ideas, the growing awareness of national affairs, and the process of modernization in the Dominican Republic. Under Trujillo, the propagation of views, ideas, and opinions was monopolized and exploited by the regime so that opinion groups lacked the freedom to articulate their interests or the channels in which to do so. In the post-Trujillo period, however, with the entire communication system free, open, and expanding, this characteristic of the dictatorship has in large measure been eliminated.

What seems to stand out again most clearly in this discussion, nevertheless, is the large impediments that prevent rapid development and modernization in the Dominican Republic. The problems of the educational system seem so large and so difficult as to be almost insurmountable. Though a new national pride and consciousness seem to be growing, Dominican culture has traditionally not served as a unifying factor in the country. And despite the rapid advances in the communications realm, it is significant that the public information media are highly partisan, at the service of one particular group and point of view or another, and thus tend to contribute to the further division rather than to the fusion of the society.

Chapter IX

THE ECONOMY

THE DOMINICAN REPUBLIC is economically poor and underdeveloped. As of 1963, the average yearly income of its people was in the neighborhood of $200 per person; but, as we have stated, even this low figure is misleading, since most of the income is concentrated in a few hands—the elite, the salaried or self-employed middle sectors, and the relatively small number of organized workers. Most Dominicans have incomes (as well as expenses) close to zero: they buy little, sell little, and subsist on the verge of starvation and death. The sheer poverty of the bulk of the people is the single most striking feature of the Dominican economy.

Although mining, manufacturing, industry, and tourism have increased in recent decades, the Dominican Republic remains basically an agricultural country. Nearly all manufacturing enterprises and industrial concerns are centered in the urban areas of Santiago and, especially, Santo Domingo; most of the rest of the country concerns itself, in one way or another, chiefly with agriculture. The bulk of the population is tied closely to the soil, and extensive land holdings signify not only wealth but also social prestige.

Although agriculture dominates the Dominican economy, the country has been forced to import basic foodstuffs. Importation of food is required principally because the agricultural sector of the economy, dominated by sugar, is oriented toward production for the world market rather than for home consumption.

The country suffers, then, from the paradox of being inherently rich agriculturally but not having enough food to feed its own population, and also of having its economy tied to the uncertainties of the world market prices for its principal exports or to the quotas established by the large importers. Fluctuations in the price for sugar or the manipulation of sugar quotas allotted to the country have for generations made and unmade Dominican governments.

During Trujillo's rule, the country was converted into a gigantic corporate fiefdom in which most of the national wealth was held directly by the lord of the fief (Trujillo himself), his family, or by a small circle of cronies and retainers. The expansion of the sugar industry and Trujillo's over-all economic policies led to greater exports and a booming gross national product (the average annual growth rate during the 1950's was 8 per cent) but had adverse effects on the economy as a whole. The effects would not have been so damaging if Trujillo had plowed this money back into the development of the nation, but much of the profit was wastefully used or siphoned off to nameless foreign bank accounts.

Trujillo's manipulation of the economy for his own purposes and profit contributed in a major way to the critical economic and social problems which befell the country upon his assassination. In mid-1961, the Dominican Republic had an empty treasury, unemployment rates that fluctuated between 30 and 50 per cent, a number of large foreign debts, declining agricultural production, and a foundering economy—to say nothing of immense social and political problems.

Since the end of the Trujillo regime, a concerted attempt has been made to develop and diversify the economy. Economic assistance and technical aid have poured in, the tax system has been reformed, rigid government austerity programs have been embarked upon, land distribution and agrarian reform were begun, business and commerce were expanded, new crops and new products were introduced, and a wide range of programs to stabilize and improve economic and social conditions were started. Substantial improvements have been made in some areas, but it is still too early to assess accurately either the potential or over-all results of these programs for the entire economy. It is certain, nevertheless, that the Dominican Republic has so far not passed through the "take-off" stage into the period of self-sustained growth.

ECONOMIC SECTORS

To reiterate, the Dominican Republic's economy is predominantly agricultural, although the number of industrial and commercial enterprises has greatly increased in the past two decades. Agriculture accounts for about nine-tenths of the country's export revenues, and about six out of ten employed Dominicans depend upon agriculture for their income. In terms of gross national product, agriculture provides some 41 per cent, commerce 17 per cent, manufacturing 15 per cent, government 7 per cent, and other sectors 20 per cent.

Agriculture

Little more than half of the total land area of the Dominican Republic is in farms. Of the total farm area, about one-quarter is used for crops and another quarter for pasture. The remaining half is covered with forests, brush, and scrub or lies fallow. Much of the land could be used more productively.

Land ownership is concentrated: about 1 per cent of the farms accounts for fully half the total farm land; 75 per cent of the farms contain only 14 per cent of the farm area. Gigantic land holdings (*latifundia*), much of which are wastefully or inefficiently exploited, and subsistence plots (*minifundia*) that are too small to be economically viable thus exist side by side. The entire agricultural sector, furthermore, remains unmechanized;

soil preparation, planting, tilling, and harvesting are still largely done by hand labor.

Trujillo was the country's largest landowner. He bought some tracts, acquired others from private owners by devious techniques, and expanded his acreage by dispossessing peasants and taking over previously unused lands. (Trujillo moved the dispossessed peasants to infertile hillsides and called this "agrarian reform.") After the collapse of the Trujillo family regime, these extensive land holdings were inherited by the government. Most of the land remained a part of the national patrimony, some was returned to its legitimate previous owners, and a small amount was distributed to landless peasants under a series of agrarian-reform programs. Still today, the government is by far the country's largest single landholder.

When Trujillo first came to power in 1930, the Dominican Republic was beginning to develop a fairly well diversified system of agriculture and farm ownership. During the last fifteen years of his rule, however, Trujillo placed great emphasis on industrialization and on increased sugar production at the expense of general agriculture. These policies resulted in increased earnings for the country (largely for Trujillo personally) but also in high social and economic costs. The increased emphasis on sugar came at a time when world prices for that product were falling; and dispossession, slave labor, tyranny, and enforced sacrifices worsened the lot of the many poor.

Sugar cane is the Dominican Republic's major crop, and the country is one of the world's leading producers and exporters of that product. The cane is grown on large plantations, transported from the fields by oxcart, truck, or small-gauge railroad, and processed in some sixteen mills located near the cane fields. Cane-growing is concentrated in the southeast, although plantations also exist near Barahona in the southwest, in the center of the island, and near Puerto Plata on the north coast. Trujillo owned twelve of the sixteen mills, and these also passed into the hands of the government upon the demise of the dictatorship. The sugar industry then became an autonomous government corporation, which, however, continued to operate at a loss because of rising costs, inefficiency, and high wage demands on the part of labor.

Cutting sugar cane by hand is hard work, and since the Dominicans consider it also demeaning, Haitians or West Indians are often brought in to supplement the labor force. The overwhelming emphasis on sugar also causes seasonal unemployment problems: during the cane-cutting season, from December to June, employment is high; during the rest of the year, it falls off sharply, and the unemployment rate may rise to half the regular working force. The importance of sugar for the Dominican economy is further underscored in the Dominican press by front-page banner headlines concerning the considerations in the Agricultural Committee of the U.S. House of Representatives, which sets quotas for the importation of sugar to the United States. Sometimes, the sugar quotas are used as levers to manipulate Dominican politics; at other times, they bear directly on the success or failure of Dominican governments.

Although sugar is by far the most important crop, others are also produced for export. Coffee is grown around Barahona and on the mountain slopes bordering the Cibao Valley. In the last decade, the earnings from this crop have also been sharply affected by declining world coffee prices. As was the case with sugar, most coffee before World War II was marketed in Europe; now, about 80 per cent is sold to the United States. In recent years, cacao has tended to replace coffee as the country's second most valuable crop. The production of both these crops is regulated by the Dominican Coffee and Cacao Institute.

Tobacco is grown in the northern part of the country around the cities of Santiago and Puerto Plata. Dominican tobacco is largely of the dark variety, has a high bouquet and full aroma, and consists of two basic types: the *criollo*, most of which is exported, and the *olor*, which is consumed locally. Though the production of rice has more than doubled since 1950, demand has outstripped production, so that the country now has to import rice. Peanuts and bananas are raised for export. Yucca, sweet potatoes, corn, yams, and fruits are grown throughout the country, primarily for local consumption.

Neither the livestock nor the fishing industry has attained major importance. Meat shortages have developed, and the dairy industry is little developed. Chickens, goats (a Dominican luxury), pigs, and cows graze freely along the roadways and have to scamper for the side as cars approach (which may help to account for the toughness of much of the meat). Also, much of the livestock is underfed or diseased. Scientific breeding and feeding techniques are only beginning to be tried.

Relatively few foreign concerns have agricultural holdings in the Dominican Republic. The largest is the U.S.-owned South Puerto Rico Sugar Company, which has extensive holdings around the city of La Romana. At one time, the United Fruit Company, through its subsidiary the Grenada Company, had banana properties in the far northwest; but United Fruit discontinued its operations completely in the 1960's. The Dominican Fruit & Steamship Company, originally established with foreign capital but later expanded with considerable Dominican participation, developed a major banana plantation on the southern coast near Azua. After the restoration of some degree of peace and order following the revolution in 1965, various major U.S. concerns became interested again in investing in the Dominican Republic.

Economic "imperialism" (that is, overwhelming foreign economic dominance) is not a major problem in the Dominican Republic, but her agriculture clearly has other problems that seem almost insoluble. The Dominican economy is essentially a one-crop economy which makes it dependent on the vagaries of the international market and foreign quotas, and, despite being overwhelmingly agricultural, the country must import basic foodstuffs. Not only is it basically an agricultural country —a hallmark of a traditional society—but agricultural production itself remains unmechanized, inefficient, and unmodern. New concepts and programs of agrarian reform, agricultural credit, farm extension services and education, soil conservation, agricultural cooperatives, irrigation, crop fertilization, farm mechanization, crop production and diversification are now being introduced, but their effects have only recently begun to be felt.

Rural Dominicans, in addition, are often reluctant to experiment with these new programs or to try new seeds or new fertilizers. For *campesinos* living on the margin of starvation, the old ways are inadequate but at least they are certain. To them, change and experimentation with new crops or methods, on the other hand, imply uncertainty, and the peasants fear that trying new and uncertain techniques may leave them worse off than before and push them over the narrow margin into starvation. Many peasants are unwilling to take the risk that experimentation implies.

Mining

Though deposits of a variety of minerals are known to exist in the Dominican Republic, few of these are now being exploited. The discovery of only a little gold by the original Spanish conquerors meant that mining was discontinued almost completely toward the mid-sixteenth century and only attained some importance again in the 1950's.

The Aluminum Company of America (Alcoa) began bauxite exploitation at Cabo Rojo, in the extreme southwest, in 1958. The ore is taken from an open pit by conveyor-belt to the ships at Alcoa piers and from there to plants in the United States. It is estimated that the deposit has reserves for 20–30 years.

In 1955, the Barium Steel Company began mining iron ore

near Cotúi in the center of the country but ceased operations three years later. A new company then began to exploit this premium ore. In 1964, another business enterprise, the Quisqueya Oil Company, signed a contract with the Dominican government to undertake oil explorations. Falconbridge Nickel Company, a Canadian concern, also obtained a concession to mine nickel ore in the mountains near Constanza.

A few other mining operations are conducted in the Dominican Republic but none of them on a large scale. Salt, oil, marble, gypsum, copper, nickel, and sulphur are all mined, but most of the deposits are small and do not contribute significantly to the country's gross national product. Furthermore, the few big mining operations that are in existence ship the ore directly outside the country for processing, with the result that the Dominican Republic receives few benefits from the exploitation of its mineral wealth in terms of more industry and manufacturing, more jobs, and a higher standard of living.

Industry

Industrialization began late in the Dominican Republic. Until the Trujillo era, the only industry of any size was sugar; and during the first decade of Trujillo's rule, few new manufacturing concerns were established. The increased demand for Dominican agricultural products, which began during World War II and continued for a decade after 1945, provided the first stimulus for industrialization. Trujillo's own wish to expand the economy rapidly, regardless of the human costs involved, was another important spur. During the 1940's and 1950's, a large number of manufacturing, industrial, and commercial enterprises—mostly Trujillo-owned—were established. Most of these, however, were fairly small-scale enterprises for the production of shoes, textiles, food items, etc.; there is still no heavy industry in the country.

Following the overthrow of the Trujillo regime in 1961, the

government inherited some eighty-seven commercial and industrial concerns that had formerly belonged to the Trujillo family and its cronies. A few of these properties, such as the newspaper *El Caribe*, were returned to private ownership, while others—some land, the taxi fleet—were distributed to poorer elements by President Balaguer in a gigantic giveaway. The bulk, however, remained in the hands of the government. Most Dominicans agree that these concerns should remain public property and be used for the betterment of the entire nation, but the country lacks the technicians and administrators to run this giant industrial complex proficiently and profitably.

A number of programs were put forward and enacted in an effort to place these government-run businesses and industries on a sound, efficient, and profitable basis. Technical and managerial help was brought in from the United States, Germany, Puerto Rico, and other countries; and early in 1962 a National Planning Board was set up. In May of that year, an Industrial Development Corporation was created as an autonomous government institution not only to run the former Trujillo properties but to serve as an investment bank and provide loans for the establishment of new industries. Foreign loans and grants were also made available.

Despite ambitious programs and considerable efforts, these government-run businesses and industries were not wholly successful. Though supposedly autonomous, they were not free from political pressures and were often employed as a kind of large pork-barrel or spoils system by which government officials could reward their friends and allies. Nepotism and corruption were prevalent. These factors, together with the lack of technical help and efficient management, labor pressures, and increasing expenses, meant that many of the businesses and industries operated at a loss. Pressures mounted for the government to return them to private ownership.

Since the end of Trujillo's rule, successive Dominican governments have also tried to encourage the establishment of new private manufacturing and industrial concerns. Although a number of new enterprises were started after 1961, and although the popular demand for finished goods has risen, governmental efforts to encourage manufacturing and industry have not been overly successful. Among the reasons for the disappointing results are political instability, the lack of a skilled labor force, the small size of the market, the lack of investment capital, and a scarcity of technicians and administrators. Hence, most major manufactured goods are not produced domestically but must be imported. The Dominican Republic has neither the mineral, the financial, nor the human base to support industrialization and manufacturing on a large scale.

Tourism

Tourism has never been a very important industry in the Dominican Republic. During the Trujillo era, three luxury hotels —the Jaragua, Hispaniola, and Embajador—were built in Santo Domingo, and a number of other smaller but equally modern hotels were built in the countryside. Trujillo also developed other tourist facilities and engaged in an extensive publicity campaign to lure more visitors to the Dominican Republic; but after an initial spurt, tourism declined as a result of the unfavorable press that Trujillo's dictatorship began to receive.

Despite the efforts of the government tourist commission, tourism did not increase greatly in the post-Trujillo period either. Elaborate—and usually unrealistic—plans were drawn up to lure visitors, but they seldom got out of the planning stage. Prices in the large hotels remained beyond all but the most lavish expense-account budgets (and were thus filled mostly with the many U.S. officials who came to work on the enormous number of economic and social-development projects begun in the post-Trujillo era), and the service usually left something to be desired. Political instability kept many potential visitors away.

Furthermore, there was little for tourists to do. The natural beauty of the island and the friendliness of its people were not sufficient to compensate for a lack of recreational facilities, of indigenous cultural attractions, and, perhaps most important, of other tourists.

Fuels, Lubricants, and Power

No coal or fuel oil is currently produced in the Dominican Republic, but wood, charcoal, bagasse (a derivative of sugar cane), and imported bottled gas are used as fuel in homes and commercial establishments. A few privately owned electric companies exist, but the electric-power output is dominated by a government-owned corporation. As the country develops, the demand for electric power is rising rapidly; but the hydroelectric potential of the Rio Yaque del Norte, the Rio Yaque del Sur, and other rivers has so far been little exploited. Early in 1968, however, plans were formulated and funds acquired for the building on the Yaque del Norte of the new Tavera dam, which has many important implications for the development of the entire Cibao.

Transportation and Marketing

Trujillo greatly improved the transportation system of the Dominican Republic. The network of primary and secondary roads he built, though in need of repair, links almost the entire country, and privately-owned trucks, buses, and passenger cars provide the chief means of transportation. Trujillo also improved the seaport facilities and expanded the merchant marine. Air transportation links the country directly with Puerto Rico, Haiti, the United States, and Venezuela, but domestic air service (not absolutely essential in a country of this small size) has only recently been developed. The only commercial railroad has fallen into disuse, and internal water transportation is seldom used because of the seasonal shallowness of most major rivers and their many rapids. Government programs for the expansion and improvement of all transportation facilities have been elaborated, but few of the plans have been put into operation or implemented.

The comparatively good primary transportation system is not matched by the marketing and storage facilities. The Dominican Republic lacks warehouses, refrigeration facilities, and farm-to-market roads. Agricultural products must frequently be brought on the backs of peasants or mules from the farms to central points, and from there they are transported to the markets over often deteriorated road surfaces. The lack of storage facilities and of farm-to-market roads frequently results in loss through spoilage. The larger towns have daily markets, but the villages may have only one market day per week. Because of high transportation costs, inefficiency, and often high costs for large numbers of intermediaries, some foods grown in the Dominican Republic sell at a higher price than the same items imported.

FOOD SUPPLY AND CONSUMPTION

The Dominican food supply is insufficient and inadequate, and most Dominicans are undernourished. Consumption levels per person, particularly during the 1950–60 decade, when Trujillo literally starved the population in order to satisfy his greed for greater personal wealth, were among the lowest in Latin America; in fact, they were well below minimum nutritional requirements. Average daily diets contain about 2,000 calories, and most diets are deficient in protein as well as in calories. Protein consumption averages about 50 pounds per person per year (of which only about 11 pounds is meat), and most of this is served on the tables of the middle and upper classes. The lack of adequate food is evidenced in the bloated bellies of many children and in the diseases caused by malnutrition of many adults.

The inadequacy of the diet of most Dominicans is chiefly due to their poverty and low purchasing power, but other factors are also involved. Habits, traditions, and lack of knowledge concerning what constitutes a good, well-balanced diet are also important. CARE officials found, for example, that some Dominicans would not eat wheat until it was processed to look like rice. Dominicans are often reluctant to eat salads and some vegetables. Furthermore, the milk, sold in the streets and ladled out from large cans, is seldom without a high bacteria count. The same is true even for bottled soft-drinks. Transportation and storage deficiencies, unmechanized and inefficient farm techniques, and the concentration on production for world markets rather than for home consumption further contribute to food shortages.

In the countryside one finds banana, mango, coffee, plantain, sapodilla, and cacao trees; and the small *bohíos* (huts) are often surrounded by small plots of rice, yucca, corn, cassava, sweet potatoes, guava bushes, and pineapple. These foods—especially rice and beans—are the mainstays of the Dominican diet. Milk, meat, eggs, cheese, and fish are expensive luxuries and are consumed only infrequently.

Prior to Trujillo's overriding concentration on sugar and the development of manufacturing and industry, the Dominican Republic had been practically self-sufficient in food production. This is not to say that food production was particularly high, however, but that consumption was low. In more recent years, the demand for food has grown, at the same time that more food has had to be imported. Since prices have risen, the poor have found it increasingly difficult to feed themselves. It seems inconceivable—notwithstanding the "law of comparative advantage"—that in an agricultural country eggs, for example, had to be imported from Mississippi and were sold at 10¢ each. To help relieve the shortages, the Catholic Relief Service, CARE, and the Church World Service have distributed surplus food, and numerous projects to improve agricultural production have been initiated. But the diet of most Dominicans remains inadequate.

FINANCE

The gold peso is the basic monetary unit of the country. Trujillo paid off the foreign debt that had plagued the Dominican Republic for decades (for which he claimed the title "Financial Emancipator of the Nation") and soundly established the peso on a par with the U.S. dollar. For most of the 1950's, the peso remained stable and easily convertible; but in recent years, it has begun to slip, and rumors of a devaluation frequently make front-page headlines. On the black market, the value of the peso may fluctuate between R.D.$1.10 and R.D.$1.30 to the U.S. dollar.

The financial life of the country is regulated and managed by the Central Bank of the Dominican Republic. Another government financial institution, the Reserve Bank, serves as both a fiscal agent and a depository for national funds. With ten branches, it is also the nation's largest commercial bank. Other government-run banks function principally as loan and development agencies, providing technical assistance and loans at considerably lower rates than those offered in the past. These include the several new savings and loan associations, the Agricultural Credit Bank, the Industrial Development Corporation, and the several newly created but not yet fully effective cooperatives and credit unions.

A number of private foreign commercial banks have branches in the Dominican Republic. They include the Chase Manhattan Bank, the First National City Bank, the Royal Bank of Canada, and the Bank of Nova Scotia. The first two, especially, are looked upon with suspicion by Dominican extreme nationalists who tend to see the specter of imperialism in all U.S.-owned concerns. Among Dominican banks, the Banco Nacional, the Credit and Savings Bank, and the Banco Popular Dominicano are also important.

There is no stock exchange or other formally constituted securities market in the Dominican Republic—largely because there are so few companies that issue common stock. Most business concerns remain individual- or family-owned and operated.

Prior to the Trujillo era, fiscal revenues as well as government expenditures were exceedingly small. The government performed few services, and its budget was correspondingly small. The major source of government funds was customs revenues; expenses went mostly for the salaries of the few public employees or for maintaining the machinery of government. A considerable share drained away for pay-offs, graft, or private expenses (such as a personal army).

During the Trujillo era, particularly after World War II, the scope of government revenues and expenses expanded greatly. Taxes were collected more regularly (although the Trujillo family properties and income were exempt), and the government found numerous other legal and illegal means to raise revenues. Expenses went into building up and maintaining the huge military apparatus, into public works, into a host of new and expanded government activities, and into the private accounts of the Trujillos. In 1958, government revenues topped R.D.$150 million for the first time.

The end of the Trujillo era caused a major disruption of the national accounts. For several years thereafter, expenses exceeded income. Property or income taxes were collected sporadically, if at all. At the same time that revenues were falling, however, demands were rising, and the government was now called upon to perform a large number of functions and provide a variety of services it had never engaged in before—agrarian reform, social security, minimum wages, development planning, cooperatives, etc. Complete financial collapse was averted only by large infusions of U.S. aid in the form of gifts and loans.

The continuing economic and financial crisis and the need for foreign loans resulted in an unfavorable balance of payments for the Dominican Republic. In an effort to remedy this imbalance, successive governments have been forced to slash government salaries, curtail wage demands on the part of labor, and instigate far-reaching austerity programs. These programs proved to be exceedingly unpopular, and they were important factors in causing the outbreak of the revolution in 1965. In the Dominican Republic, economic vicious circles are closely intertwined with political ones.

The conflict between the need to consume and the need to invest has also torn the Dominican system. Trujillo had achieved one of the highest ratios of capital formation to gross national product in Latin America through the techniques of strict political centralization and dictatorship, economic monopoly, and exploitation of the population. He could thus maintain a high level of investment, though the resulting profits went more often into his own pocket than into projects beneficial to the entire nation. Furthermore, private initiative by those outside the ruling clique was stifled, and profitable enterprises were quickly snatched up by the regime. As Trujillo faced the crises of the last two years of his rule, both public and private investment began to contract.

In the post-Trujillo period, consumption generally took precedence over investment. While this was clearly more humane than the Trujillo policy, it also meant that there was less capital available for investment in development projects. The country thus stood little chance of breaking through into the stage of self-sustained growth. Political instability, furthermore, not only frightened away foreign investment (which totaled $110 million in 1961, of which about 98 per cent came from the U.S.), but also led the Dominicans with savings to invest their money in Puerto Rico, the United States, or Europe, where it could obviously do the Dominican Republic little good. No just and workable formula for solving the investment-versus-consumption dilemma has as yet been found.

FOREIGN TRADE

In the past three decades, as the Dominican economy has expanded, sharp increases have been registered in the country's foreign trade. Though the volume of trade steadily increased, export earnings fluctuated because of changing world market prices for Dominican products, especially sugar. As Trujillo, in the face of growing opposition during the last two years of his rule, sought to strengthen his regime, imports were sharply curtailed; and because of the diplomatic and economic sanctions imposed by the Organization of American States, new markets had to be found for Dominican exports.

Since the end of the Trujillo regime, both exports and imports have increased rapidly. Sugar remains the principal export commodity, but coffee, cacao, chocolate, tobacco, bananas, molasses, and bauxite are also exported. The chief imports are food and, of course, manufactured goods. Almost all major items—furniture, appliances, automobiles, machinery—as well as many specialized smaller items, like baby food, must be imported—and usually reach the market at prohibitive prices.

The country's foreign trade is principally with the United States. Prior to World War I, trade with Europe was extensive— Dominican tobacco was used in the well-known French Gauloise cigarettes, its cacao went into German and Swiss chocolate, and sugar was marketed in Great Britain. Little of this trade is left; today, the United States, with some 70–80 per cent of the market, is the Dominican Republic's leading supplier and customer. The European and Asian nations are interested in the country as a market for their exported goods, however, and European cars and Japanese transistor radios are popular. But it is likely that the Dominican Republic will remain, economically as it is politically, closely tied to the United States.

The volume of Dominican trade with the rest of Latin America amounts to only about 2–3 per cent of the total. The idea that the Dominican Republic should join the movement toward Latin American economic integration by becoming more closely associated with Puerto Rico and possibly with the Central American Common Market is, however, gaining ground.

GOVERNMENT INVOLVEMENT IN THE ECONOMY

Traditionally, the Dominican government has played a minor role in the planning and development of the economy. And during the Trujillo dictatorship, no over-all program for national development existed. Rather, the profits from the Trujillo era went largely to benefit the ruling group, primarily the dictator himself. The so-called Trujillo Plan was more a program of spectacular public works than of a well-conceived plan for economic modernization. Nevertheless, Trujillo's rule, by employing severely dictatorial methods, also raised enough capital to construct projects necessary for the future development of the country—port facilities, highways, airports, communications, etc.

Since 1962, the government has played an increasingly important role in the promotion of economic development. A National Planning Board was established by the Council of State to supervise the economic and social development programs, coordinate the plans of the various ministries and agencies, and advise the government on the progress made. During Bosch's tenure, the Inter-American Center of Social Studies (CIDES), headed by Sacha Volman and backed by U.S. funds, performed many of the same functions. Today, regulation of the

economy and planning for development are accepted governmental practices in the Dominican Republic.

The government became active in almost all spheres of the
economy. The Industrial Development Corporation was formed
to exercise control over the former Trujillo properties. An Agrarian Institute was set up to provide for the redistribution of land
and a number of related programs, such as rural housing, super-
vised agricultural credit, technical assistance to farmers, installation of irrigation and electrification projects, and the construction
of roads. A Cattle Institute, Coffee and Cacao Institute, Cooperative Institute, and a number of other government-run but
supposedly autonomous agencies were established to promote
further development.

As the government's regulatory and development programs
increased, the scope of its public functions and responsibilities
also expanded and far surpassed those of the private sector. The
Dominican government is easily the country's largest spender,
buyer, employer, and businessman. In addition to the huge
civil service and the large number of development institutes,
the government runs sugar mills, the wheat mill, the chocolate
factory, the beer factory, the electrical plant, and a wide variety
of other public corporations. Successive governments and an
increasing number of able, young economists connected with the
various government banks and financial institutions have seen
the need for a managed, mixed economy and have laid the preliminary groundwork for a progressive and integrated national
development program. The implementation of these plans and
ideas, however, has not been very successful; and the Dominican Republic remains one of the few Latin American countries
which has not submitted a comprehensive development plan to
the Alliance for Progress. The emergency atmosphere created by
constant political and economic crises together with the rapid
changeover of governments (and hence of plans, personnel, and

programs) have prevented the various economic and social development schemes from being effectively carried out.

OUTLOOK

The Dominican Republic is, then, potentially a rich country, at least agriculturally. It has a productive land base, a favorable climate, sufficient rainfall, and an adequate labor supply. It lacks sufficient investment capital; trained technicians and administrative personnel; adequate food, housing, and health facilities; and an effective over-all development program. It is caught in a number of economic and political vicious circles from which there seems little chance to escape.

Numerous attempts have been made in the post-Trujillo era to expand and diversify the economy. New crops were introduced, and new industrial and manufacturing concerns were encouraged. Of particular importance to the future of the economy were the far-reaching new programs for agrarian reform and industrial development. Also significant were the projects for providing credit, development services, agricultural extension, education, and research. A large number of plans, programs, and projects were formulated and undertaken; yet, none of them proved to be particularly effective. The Dominican Republic remains a poor and underdeveloped land.

As it reaches the end of the decade, the country has still not pulled out of the disastrous economic decline that began in the mid-to-late 1950's. The Dominican Republic was the only Latin American nation whose revenues from exports had actually declined in the first half of the 1960's. Despite the massive infusions of foreign economic assistance and the enormous efforts on the part of Dominicans, U.S. AID officials, and various international agencies, the condition of life of most Dominicans did not seem to have improved from ten years previously —and survey data reveal that many of the people despairingly recognized the hopelessness of their plight. Economic growth barely kept pace with the population increase, and the impression grew that the entire economy and the lot of the people were slipping backward rather than getting better. Conditions worsened even more as a result of the revolution, civil war, and U.S. intervention of 1965; and, although there are some hopeful signs, it remains uncertain whether the government of Balaguer can succeed in stimulating an over-all integrative development program.

The major causes of the economic decline, it may be suggested, were political—the uncertainty and rapaciousness of the last years of Trujillo's dictatorship, the weakness of governmental and political institutions, the imbalance of the political system, the ineffectiveness of governmental programs, and the instability of the period following the Generalissimo's death. It is to these overriding political factors in the process of development and modernization that we turn next.

Chapter X

GOVERNMENTAL STRUCTURES

WE ARE USED to thinking of underdeveloped countries in economic and social terms—that is, of countries where poverty is widespread and the economy is stagnant, where large gaps exist between rich and poor, where educational facilities are limited and illiteracy is widespread, and where starvation, disease, and malnutrition are prevalent. But countries may also be politically underdeveloped—that is, countries where governmental institutions are weak and unstable, where political norms and behavior are more traditional than modern, where the government is not accepted by large blocs of the population, where political parties and interest associations are nonexistent or only in their infancy, where normal political processes do not function adequately, where governmental decisions and policies are ineffective, and where the entire political system is so tenuous that it may collapse into revolution and civil war. In these countries, also, the gap between the formal-legal-constitutional structure and actual governmental practices may be far wider than in politically more developed countries.

The Dominican Republic has many of the characteristics of an underdeveloped political system. In this chapter we shall be looking at the country's formal governmental structures—constitutions and constitutionalism, political institutions, the public service, and law and the legal system. In subsequent chapters we shall examine the more informal aspects of the political process and consider governmental decisions and policies.

CONSTITUTIONS
AND CONSTITUTIONALISM

The Dominican Republic has had a large number of constitutions. Indeed, with twenty-nine constitutions in a century and a quarter of independent history, the country is second to few nations of the world in the number of constitutions that have been promulgated. The apparent large turnover is not so great as it may seem, however, because of the Dominican practice of promulgating the document as a new constitution whenever an amendment is enacted. While technically different, most Dominican constitutions have contained in reality only minor modifications from those which were in effect before; and sweeping constitutional innovations have only recently appeared.

The existence of so many basic laws in Dominican history implies a fundamental lack of agreement—or consensus— among Dominicans on the "rules of the game" that should regulate the political system. Most Dominican governments have felt compelled to write a new constitution and to change the rules of the game to fit their own wishes. Not only have successive governments often violently disagreed with the policies and programs of their predecessors, but they have frequently rejected completely the political framework within which their predecessors operated. Constitutionalism—loyalty to a set of governing principles rather than to the person who promulgates them—has become a matter of overriding importance in the Dominican Republic only in most recent years.

The chaotic revolution of 1965 was made still more confusing by reports that, at one and the same time, referred to one side as the "rebels" or "Constitutionalists" and to the other as the "loyalists" or "anti-Constitutionalists." Later, it became clear, however, that the issue of "constitutionalism" and the principles for which this term served as a symbol were among the most important of the revolution—perhaps even more important than any of the personalities or groups involved in the conflict. For the revolution was not simply a conflict among those who disputed as to how the formal structure of government should be organized. Rather, the recent constitutions of the Dominican Republic had come to represent widely divergent ways of life and wholly different beliefs as to the method of structuring the good society—ideas and arrangements which were so divergent that they had caused the revolution to break out in the first place.

The Dominican Constitution of 1962 had been promulgated by the Council of State. As such, it represented to many Dominicans the elite, oligarchic elements that had governed during this period. It symbolized the *status quo* and the business-oriented, go-slow attitude of the conservative National Civic Union, many of whose members were prominent in the Council of State government.

The Constitution of 1962 also became a symbol of Trujilloism. Though the dictatorship had been overthrown in 1961, the Trujillo constitution remained in effect, changed only in particulars providing for the transfer of power to the interim Council of State and setting the dates for elections and the installation of a legitimately elected government. The Constitution of 1962 continued to be a reminder of the Trujillo dictatorship—not just of the abuses of constitutionalism which the regime practiced but also of the terrorism, corruption, fear, tyranny, thought control, murder, crime, torture, and so forth which the entire Trujillo era now represented. As a symbolic document, both of the do-nothing oligarchy and of the Trujillo dictatorship, the Constitution of 1962 aroused bitter, deep-seated, and widespread opposition, and it was not well suited to the wants and needs of the people whose government it was supposed to order.

Juan Bosch and his Dominican Revolutionary Party interpreted their overwhelming victory in the 1962 elections as a mandate to enact a wide range of reforms which would be far-reaching and revolutionary but at the same time peaceful and democratic. The country thus needed a new, revolutionary constitution as well. As Bosch stated: "The people voted for us not because I have gray hair and blue eyes but because of the ideas of the Party. . . . These ideas were revolutionary . . . and there cannot be a democratic revolution in this country if we do not have a revolutionary constitution which will permit us to make revolutionary laws."

The revolutionary Constitution of 1963, as drafted by the PRD-dominated Congress, did not differ substantially from the previous constitution insofar as the mechanics of government were concerned—the powers of the executive, legislature, and judiciary were virtually unchanged. Where it did differ radically from all previous constitutions in Dominican history was in its emphasis on the state as a positive force in promoting social justice. In keeping with the Bosch administration's orientation, the 1963 Constitution committed the government to far-reaching social reforms; in specific detail it drew a blueprint for the establishment of a democratic welfare state.

While most of the reforms contained in the Constitution were certainly needed and long overdue, they severely frightened the country's powerful vested interests. The Church objected to the articles that sanctioned divorce, secular education, and common-law marriage, as well as to the fact that it contained no specific statement identifying the Dominican Republic as a Catholic country or recognizing the 1954 Concordat that Trujillo had signed with the Vatican. The business, professional, and land-owning elite was concerned about the stress on public as opposed to private interests, the limitations on land ownership, the vague phrases concerning private property, and the many articles that favored labor at the expense of employers. The armed forces were apparently fearful that the articles providing for military subordination to civilian authority might be taken literally. Faced with the opposition of three of the most powerful groups in Dominican society, constitutional government quickly fell. The Trujillistic and oligarchic Constitution of 1962 was then restored.

The constitutions of 1962 and 1963 served, then, as symbols around which many of the conflicts of the 1965 revolution revolved. The Constitutionalists favored the restoration of the 1963 basic law, while the opposition junta forces branded it as "godless and Communistic." For the Constitutionalists, the 1962 document symbolized the corruption, tyranny, and oppression of *trujillismo* and the oligarchy, while that of 1963 represented freedom, democracy, and the prospect of social justice. The constitutions of 1962 and 1963 not only represented conflicting ideas concerning governmental structures and institutions but symbolized wholly different and opposed conceptions of society, sets of values, and ways of life.

The differences between the combatants in the revolution concerning the two constitutions were so deep and bitter that the issue was not immediately resolved. No bases for negotiations —let alone agreement—could be found, for the constitutions of 1962 and 1963 defined in written form the basic disputes between the two factions. Postponing an either-or decision on the constitutional question until an elected government could deal with it, the two sides agreed to an Act of Reconciliation and an Institutional Act. Under these acts, Héctor García Godoy served as interim president.

After Balaguer and his Partido Reformista won the 1966 elections, a call for a new constitution was promptly issued. The debate in the Constituent Assembly between the minority PRD representatives, who wanted to follow the 1963 model closely, and Balaguer's Reformistas was often sharp, but the views of the minority were listened to and often incorporated in the text, and the entire process of constitutional promulgation was accomplished peacefully and within a democratic framework.

As President Balaguer stated, the new constitution was "realistic," "a product of the national history," "progressive but not utopian." It had a long section on social justice for the poor but did not threaten the vested interests. It contained an article condemning foreign intervention in national affairs but also one prohibiting subversive propaganda. In fact, it found either a middle ground or remained silent on almost all the issues that had proven so controversial in the 1962 and 1963 documents. Although no one can yet say with certainty what impact it will have on the political process and to what degree it will be accepted by the various sectors active in the nation's politics, the Constitution of 1966—moderate, reformist but not revolutionary, democratic but acceptable to the more traditional groups—seems to many Dominicans to provide hope for the success of constitutional government in their country.

THE INSTITUTIONS OF GOVERNMENT

In many ways the Constitution of 1966 and the institutions of government established by it do not differ greatly from those established by earlier nineteenth- or twentieth-century Dominican constitutions. Thus, the introductory articles state that the national government is essentially civil, republican, democratic, and representative. Sovereignty rests with the people from whom all the powers of the state emanate. The national territory is inalienable, and Santo Domingo is designated the capital. An impressive list of civil and political rights is included. The government is divided into the familiar three branches: executive, legislative, and judicial. The Constitution declares that these three powers are independent in the exercise of their respective functions.

The Executive Branch

In practice, the executive is the dominant branch of the government, and all other governmental institutions are subservient to it. The president's powers derive from his supreme authority over national administration, the armed forces, and all public affairs. The president is also the chief beneficiary of the trend, found the world over, toward centralized decision-making and increased executive dominance. The political culture of Dominican society—with its emphasis on the *líder, machismo,* and individualism—also tends to make the presidency the focal point of national affairs. Traditionally, Dominican presidents even in the nineteenth century were strong, forceful, or charismatic leaders; and it is interesting that when governing power devolves upon a ruling group—the Council of State or the Triumvirate—a single individual (Rafael Bonnelly or Reid Cabral, respectively) always stands out.

Executive power is vested in a president, who is elected by direct vote and whose term of office is four years. In order to be president, a candidate must be a Dominican citizen by birth or origin, at least 30 years old, in possession of all political and civil rights, and must not have been in the military or the police for at least one year prior to his election. Vice-presidential candidates must meet the same qualifications. The 1966 Constitution does not bar re-election.

The vice-president may assume the office of president when the latter is ill, outside the country, or otherwise unable to perform his duties. If the president dies or is permanently unable to carry out the functions of his office, the vice-president serves until the next scheduled election. If the vice-president is also unable to fill the office, the president of the Supreme Court (who is chosen by the Senate) serves temporarily. Within fifteen days, he must convoke the National Assembly (both houses of the

Congress), which must then pick a presidential substitute to fill out the term.

The powers of the president are spelled out in twenty-seven paragraphs. Among the more important powers are those that authorize him (1) to appoint and remove cabinet ministers, sub-cabinet ministers and other public officials whose appointments are not set by the Constitution; (2) to promulgate the laws and resolutions of the Congress; (3) to name or remove members of the diplomatic corps, with the Senate's approval; (4) to receive foreign chiefs of state and their representatives; (5) to fill vacancies in the courts and the electoral tribunal when Congress is not in session, subject to retroactive approval by the Senate; (6) to arrest or expel foreigners whose activities are prejudicial to public order and good customs or to prohibit the entrance of undesirables; and (7) to command, determine the number of, and deploy the armed forces and to appoint the military chiefs. The president can also engage in direct diplomatic negotiations and conclude treaties with foreign nations, subject to Congressional approval. He may take the measures necessary to defend the nation in case of an actual or imminent armed attack by a foreign nation but must inform Congress of the measures taken. After authorization by Congress, he may also declare war and negotiate peace.

The president's emergency powers are also extensive. If Congress is not in session and the public peace is disturbed, the president may declare a state of siege and suspend the exercise of individual rights, or in case of a grave and imminent threat to national sovereignty, he may declare a national emergency. In case of public calamity, he may designate the afflicted areas as disaster zones. Should the public order, the security of the state, or the functioning of public services be threatened or the development of economic activities be impeded because of the abuse or violation of certain rights, the president may provisionally adopt the police and security measures necessary to meet the emergency. In these situations, he must, however, inform the Congress of his actions.

The limitations on presidential power are not great. They are derived chiefly from several provisions that require him to obtain Congressional consent in making certain appointments, exercising emergency powers, negotiating treaties, and entering into certain contracts. These provisions would not be likely to limit presidential discretion, however, since the nature of Dominican voting procedures ensures the president almost automatically of a majority in Congress. The president must submit an annual message to Congress that must be accompanied by reports of his ministers on their activities. The president is also held accountable to Congress for revenue and budget matters. He may not leave the country for more than fifteen days without Congressional approval and may not resign without formally doing so before the National Assembly. These limitations do not substantially reduce the president's over-all power.

The Constitution of 1966 also provides for ministers and sub-cabinet ministers to assist in the execution of public administrative functions. These officials must be Dominican citizens, at least 25 years of age, and with full civil and political rights. Naturalized citizens may be ministers or sub-ministers if they have been Dominican citizens for at least ten years. The powers of the ministries are determined by law and not set forth in the Constitution, but the president is constitutionally responsible for the actions of his ministers.

The presidency is clearly the focal point of the government. The importance of this position is such that a great deal depends on whether the country has an able chief executive and on the orientation of the person holding the office. Trujillo, an astute and clever Machiavellian, concentrated all power in his own hands and ruled as a dictator for thirty-one years. Juan Bosch sought to effect a democratic revolution in the Dominican Republic; but he was not so able an administrator or so realistic a politician, and his well-intentioned reform programs collapsed when his government was so quickly overthrown. Balaguer, though not a strong or charismatic personality, has proved to be exceedingly clever as a politician and has generally steered a middle course. In any case, because of the extensive powers that go with the office and because much of the national life swirls around it, the Dominican presidency is a particularly important prize.

The Legislature

The 1966 Constitution confers all legislative powers on the Congress of the Republic, which consists of a Senate and a Chamber of Deputies. The offices of senator and deputy are incompatible with all other public offices. If vacancies occur, the political party that originally occupied the seat submits a list of three names to the corresponding chamber, which then selects one to fill the vacancy. If the party does not submit a list, the chamber may itself choose a successor.

The election of senators and deputies is by direct vote every four years. One senator is elected from each of the twenty-six provinces and from the National District, making a total of twenty-seven. Deputies are also elected in the provinces and the National District, one deputy being elected for each 50,000 inhabitants or fraction of more than 25,000; no province may have less than two deputies. Currently, there are seventy-four representatives in the Chamber of Deputies.

Deputies and senators must be Dominican citizens, at least 25 years old, with full civil and political rights. They must also be natives or residents of the province in which they are running for at least five consecutive years. Naturalized citizens are eligible for Congress if they have been Dominican citizens for at least ten years and have resided in the province in which they are running for five years.

The Senate and Chamber of Deputies meet together as the National Assembly on specific occasions cited by the Constitution—for example, when both the president and vice-president are unable to fill their terms and a successor must be designated. More than half of each chamber must be present, and decisions are made by an absolute majority vote. Ordinarily, however, the chambers meet separately. Decisions in each chamber are also made by an absolute majority vote—except on matters previously declared "urgent," which require a two-thirds vote.

The exclusive powers of each chamber are limited, but the powers of the whole Congress are fairly extensive. The Senate (1) selects the members of the Supreme Court and of the lower courts; (2) chooses the president and the members of the Supreme Electoral Tribunal and the accounting office; (3) approves diplomatic appointments made by the president; and (4) judges accusations brought before it by the Chamber of Deputies against elected public officials for misconduct or neglect in the exercise of their duties. (A three-fourths vote is needed for a conviction, and the penalty cannot exceed deprivation of office.) The only exclusive power of the Chamber of Deputies is to bring accusations against public officials before the Senate. Such an accusation requires the support of a three-fourths vote of the total membership.

Under the Constitution, the Congress as a whole has broad authority. This includes the power to: (1) levy taxes and determine the means of their collection and handling; (2) create or abolish provinces, municipalities, or other political divisions of the territory; (3) declare a state of siege in a locality where disturbances of the peace or public catastrophes occur, or a state of national emergency in the event of a threat to the national sovereignty; (4) regulate immigration; (5) determine the number of courts of appeal and create or abolish regular and special courts; (6) approve or reject extraordinary expenditures requested by the executive; (7) legislate on all matters concerning the public debt; (8) decree the necessity of constitutional reform; (9) examine annually all acts of the executive and approve them if they conform with the constitution and the laws; (10) grant amnesty for political causes; (11) interrogate ministers on matters within their jurisdictions; and (12) legislate on all matters not within the authority of another branch of the state or contrary to the Constitution.

Bills may be introduced by senators, deputies, the president, the Supreme Court (in judicial matters), and the Supreme Electoral Tribunal (in electoral matters). Each measure must be discussed on two separate days with an interval of at least one day between. (Only if a particular bill has previously been declared urgent may it be discussed on two consecutive days.) A bill passed by one chamber then goes to the other, where the same procedures are observed. If amendments are made in the second chamber, the measure is returned to the chamber in which it was introduced. If this chamber accepts the amendments, the bill goes to the executive. If not, the measure, including the objections, is again sent to the second chamber. If this body now approves, the bill is sent to the executive. If not, it is considered rejected.

Bills approved by both houses and signed by the president become law. If the president does not approve, the bill is sent back to the chamber where it originated and is discussed again. If both houses of Congress subsequently approve it by a two-thirds vote, the bill becomes law regardless of presidential disapproval. The president is then required to promulgate and publish the bill, and it becomes the official law of the land. In practice, however, it is doubtful that Congress would act contrary to presidential wishes, since the president dominates the legislature.

The Judiciary

Judicial power is exercised by the Supreme Court of Justice and by other courts created by the Constitution and by law. The Constitution establishes courts of first instance, in each province, a land tribunal, and courts of appeal. Justices of the peace exist in each municipality and in the National District. The Constitution also sets up a court of accounts that examines the finances of the Republic and reports to Congress. Like its law and legal system, the judicial organization of the Dominican Republic is based on the French model.

The Supreme Court consists of nine judges, although a quorum, as established by law, is sufficient for it to deliberate and render judgments. The Senate chooses the judges on the Supreme Court as well as those of the other courts. Supreme Court justices must be Dominican by birth or origin and at least 35 years of age, enjoy full political and civil rights, have a law degree, and have practiced law or held judicial office for at least twelve years. The qualifications for judges in the lower courts, from the courts of appeal and the land court to the courts of first instance and the justices of the peace, become progressively less strict.

The Supreme Court has the exclusive power to: (1) take jurisdiction in cases involving the president, vice-president, senators, deputies, ministers, vice-ministers, fellow judges of the Supreme Court and judges of the lower courts, and members of the diplomatic corps; (2) act as a court of cassation; (3) serve as the court of last instance on matters forwarded from the appellate courts; (4) exercise final disciplinary action, including suspension or dismissal, over all members of the judiciary; and (5) transfer justices from one jurisdiction to another to ensure better judicial administration. The Supreme Court does not have the power to review the constitutionality of laws, decrees, or resolutions; and, in practice, the entire judicial branch is not independent and co-equal but subservient to the government in power. Frequently, moreover, politics dominates the court proceedings; and the entire judicial system is subject to outside pressures and even intimidation.

Local Government

The Dominican Republic, which also bases its system of local government on the French model, is divided into twenty-six provinces plus a National District; the provinces, in turn, are subdivided into seventy-seven municipalities. Each province is governed by a civil governor appointed by the president. (Balaguer made front-page headlines throughout the hemisphere when he appointed women as governors in all twenty-six provinces.) A governor must be a Dominican, at least 25 years old, and in full possession of his civil and political rights. The Constitution states that his powers and duties are determined by law.

The municipalities and the National District are governed by mayors and municipal councils who are popularly elected for four-year terms. The size of the council depends on the population of the district, but there must be at least five members. The qualifications of municipal officials as well as the functions, powers, and duties of mayors and councils are determined by law. Naturalized citizens may hold municipal office provided they have lived in the municipality for at least ten years.

Beginning in 1962, an attempt was made to strengthen Dominican local government. A new, more effective municipal league came into existence and efforts were made to develop community spirit, local initiative, and self-help projects. These attempts were not wholly successful, in large part because there is little tradition of local government in the Dominican Republic. The national government in Santo Domingo remains the focus of the country's affairs, and provincial and local governments continue to depend on the central authority for almost all affairs and undertakings.

Elections

Voting in the Dominican Republic is free, secret, personal, and obligatory for both men and women. A special feature of the electoral system is that when two or more posts are to be filled, the minority is guaranteed representation. Those who are at least eighteen years old (or married) are eligible to vote; there is no literacy requirement. Only members of the police and of the armed forces and those who have lost their citizenship or whose rights as citizens have been suspended (such as criminals) may not vote. Elections are regulated by law and administered by the Supreme Electoral Tribunal and by sub-tribunals established by it. The two general elections and one municipal election since Trujillo's fall have, by and large, been fair and honest. Elections, however, still represent only one of several means to power in the Dominican Republic and do not necessarily convey the definitive sense of legitimacy that is usually accorded an elected government in the more developed democratic nations.

The Armed Forces

According to the Constitution, the armed forces are essentially obedient to the civil power and apolitical; they do not have the power to deliberate on laws. Their constitutionally-assigned duties are to defend the independence and integrity of the Republic, to maintain public order, and to uphold the Constitution and the laws. At the president's discretion, the armed forces may participate in programs of civic action and of social and economic development. In fact, however, the activities of the armed forces have often been extraconstitutional; the military tends to view itself as the ultimate arbiter of national political affairs.

General Provisions

Among the miscellaneous articles included in the 1966 Constitution are those designating national holidays, describing the flag, condemning privilege and prohibiting titles of nobility, providing that political parties and groups may organize in accord with the law and the Constitution, promising sanctions against those who use public office for personal gain, and stating that the artistic and historical as well as mineral wealth of the country are part of the national cultural patrimony and belong to the state.

The institutions established by the Constitution of 1966 appear to be well conceived—at least on paper. Constitutionalism, however, has not had a long or very glorious history in the Dominican Republic. The political institutions established by the most recent Constitution are generally weak and often ineffectual, and the practices and guidelines contained in the new basic law are largely untried and not fully accepted by the people. Indeed, most of the constitutional measures represent goals and aspirations for the society to achieve and do not always correspond to actual operating procedures. There is as yet no basic consensus in the Dominican Republic on the rules of the game—on the institutions and practices written into the Constitution. The country's entire decision-making apparatus remains uncertain and tenuous and may be considered wholly illegitimate by a sizable proportion of the population.

THE PUBLIC SERVICE

The fall of the Trujillo dictatorship in 1961 did not mean that the traditions and practices of that era also ceased. Corruption, nepotism, wholesale dismissals for purely political reasons, loyalty checks, and the sowing of distrust and suspicion had become ingrained habits and did not disappear overnight, as Trujillo did. The old habits were, however, challenged by newer forces—austerity programs, the emergence of a government workers' organization, the efforts to enact a civil service law, the "de-Trujilloization" campaign, and the expanded government services. The clash between the traditional style of bureaucratic behavior and the new demands and forces contributed significantly to the political instability of the post-Trujillo period.

As formally organized, the president's cabinet consists of ten ministers of state. Making up almost a fourth branch of government are the fourteen autonomous agencies that are intertwined with the executive and its ministries through numerous connecting committees and informal arrangements. (See chart, page 168.) Even excluding those employed in the numerous autonomous agencies and the thousands of seasonal cane-cutters who work in the state-owned sugar complexes, the government is the nation's largest employer. In 1963, a study placed the number of government employees at 50,000.

The physical appearance of the governmental apparatus is impressive, since many of the departments and agencies are housed in the luxurious mansions that once belonged to Trujillo. The most imposing collection of government buildings is the one that was originally constructed in 1955 for the former dictator's Peace Fair. Located on the Caribbean shore some 3 miles west of downtown Santo Domingo, the complex of seventy-nine structures is the center of much of the government's activities.

The model physical appearance of the buildings is not necessarily matched by operational efficiency. Electrical wires as well as lines of command meander haphazardly, and there is an almost complete lack of organization. The paperwork is excessive, but the mountains of papers are not efficiently stored or handled and frequently pile up in the courtyard. Most government employees work six hours a day (7:30 A.M–1:30 P.M.), five

FORMAL STRUCTURE OF THE DOMINICAN GOVERNMENT*

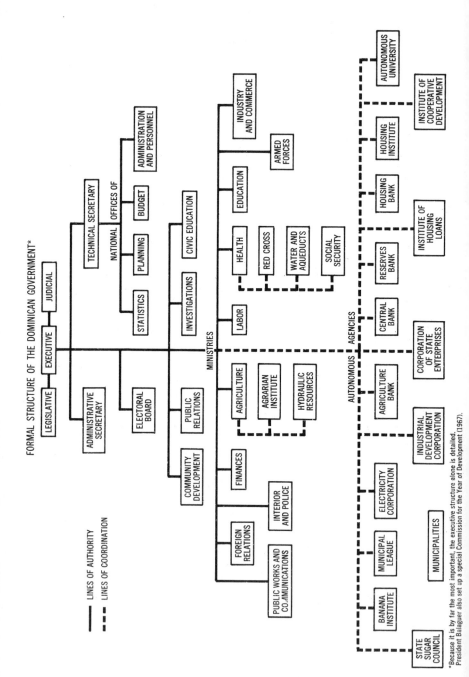

LINES OF AUTHORITY
LINES OF COORDINATION

*Because it is by far the most important, the executive structure alone is detailed.
President Balaguer also set up a special Commission for the Year of Development (1967).

days a week. Only in the tourist office are routine matters handled speedily (this may be a legacy of the Trujillo regime). For the most part, the picture is one of lethargy, long coffee breaks, a great deal of talking and banter, little work, and much inefficiency.

A visit to the National Palace provides a glimpse at the style of Dominican politics. Everyone knows everyone else personally or as a relative. Waiters pass in and out of the inner sanctums with little cups of coffee (*cafecitos*) on silver trays, as if government were little more than a constant series of family reunions. Indeed, favoritism to one's relatives and friends and self-aggrandizement from public projects are almost accepted norms.

The more elegantly dressed of those waiting outside the offices may hope to see an uncle or second cousin who will grant their request. One family is liable to have a near monopoly in one government department or agency (for example, eleven members of a single family once worked in the central office of the Ministry of Education and Fine Arts), and relatives receive preferential treatment. The less favored men and women sitting in the anterooms are kept waiting endlessly, and they can only hope to pounce on an official as he passes through the halls. For those fortunate enough to have good connections, government thus becomes the vehicle through which privileges and favoritism are distributed; close friends and relatives entrenched in administrative positions customarily serve as the instruments of illegal advantage. Juan Bosch, who was not a member of the Dominican elite and who was scrupulously honest, could not and would not function in this atmosphere of family favoritism and conflict-of-interest corruption, and the fact that his regime failed to conform to these accepted modes of behavior may have been an important reason why it was so quickly overthrown.

Corruption takes many different forms in the Dominican

Republic. Some government officials receive salaries without rendering any services. Outright bribes, however, occur infrequently. More important is the spirit of fraud that characterizes many government dealings—the enrichment of favored individuals through the expenditure of funds for public projects, self-aggrandizement through one's knowledge of pending government programs, contraband activities, and the receipt of goods, favors, or money through the performance of an official duty. The Dominican military is probably the greatest offender, but the civil service does not lag very far behind.

Many of the Dominican government's problems stem from the impossibility of finding and recruiting enough trained personnel to fill the many posts. In a country where the government is by far the largest employer, the problem of staffing the public service is apparent, from minor municipal posts to the presidency. In the post-Trujillo era, the United States and many international agencies sent technicians, administrators, managers, businessmen, and bureaucrats, but there were never enough to handle the growing number of activities the government was being called upon to perform. In the entire nation there were only three Dominicans with degrees in business administration. German technicians, for example, were brought in to run the country's only paper mill. The establishment of government programs and agencies in public health, housing, education, land reform, economic development, and social welfare beginning in 1962, and the expansion of these services and programs during the Bosch administration, meant that the country required an even greater quantity of qualified personnel.

Bosch's short-lived government illustrated the seriousness of the problem of effecting much-needed social reforms without adequate administrative machinery. His administration was estranged from the traditional rulers of the country and was forced to depend on well-meaning but totally inexperienced young people, political hacks, and a catchall of provincial lawyers, rural shopkeepers, and schoolteachers. To rely on the bureaucracy left over from the period of the Council of State would have meant the frustration of Bosch's reform program, but there were also not enough competent people in his own party to fill the required positions. Bosch attempted single-handedly to make up for this skilled-manpower deficit, but he could not be a one-man government, and, indeed, his own administrative ability was limited. Bosch was never able to gain the help of the small but powerful elite whose technical skills and managerial experience were necessary for the smooth running of the governmental machinery. The dilemma was not only to find enough capable leaders but also to staff the government with political allies who would be willing to scrap old ways and carry out the needed reforms.

Dominican governments have often felt (with a good deal of justification) that only those personally loyal to the national leadership can be entrusted with public charges. Emphasis is thus placed more on personal loyalty than on ability or competence, and every government (there were twelve in the first five years after Trujillo's ouster) feels compelled to dismiss those who had served a previous administration and to bring in its own full slate of office-fillers. Again, the result is enormous waste and inefficiency.

While on the one hand the post-Trujillo governments tried to find trained and experienced personnel, they were on the other hand trying to de-Trujilloize the bureaucracy. The campaign to rid the government of close collaborators with the former dictatorship, reminiscent of Germany's denazification following World War II, worked at cross purposes with the effort to find sufficient personnel to staff it. A national committee of de-Trujilloization was created; but it was soon recognized that a thorough purge would result in the dismissal of the small number of talented and experienced personnel who were so sorely needed to man the expanding government services.

President Balaguer illustrated the dilemma with the story of one of the country's most popular composers who was censured for writing *merengues* in honor of Trujillo. The composer admitted writing the *merengues* but pointed out in his defense that everyone else was equally guilty for having danced to them. No one was dismissed as a result of the de-Trujilloization committee's investigations, and the campaign to rid the public service of Trujillo collaborators soon died.

As a response to the de-Trujilloization campaign and to the fear that constant political upheavals would mean job insecurity, the government workers formed an independent civil-service association—for the first time in the nation's history. The National Federation of Public Employees and Employees of Autonomous Agencies (FENEPIA) was organized in 1961 and, at the height of its power, claimed to have 200 affiliated unions with 20,000 members in almost every ministry and department in all parts of the country. In its program, FENEPIA defended the government worker's right to be retained in his job irrespective of his party affiliation and pleaded for the advancement of democracy, the betterment of working conditions for its members, and the recognition of its members' professional status. Although claiming to be apolitical, FENEPIA often worked closely with the extreme left and was largely destroyed in 1963 by President Bosch. It was later revived, but the government workers remained largely without an effective organized voice to present their point of view and without an effective civil service law to protect them in their jobs.

The wide variety of autonomous and semi-autonomous state agencies established in the post-Trujillo years also raised many difficult questions and problems for the country. Some of these agencies dealt with a variety of social services, such as public health, education, and social security; others performed regulatory or administrative functions, such as the Sugar Council or the Central Bank. (See page 168.) Politics and corruption were rampant. In an effort to overcome these problems, President Bosch centralized control, but this produced disruption, administrative and personal rivalries, and inefficiency. The government has until today remained committed to the concept of autonomy for many state operations in order to free them from political harassment and interference, but this has frequently also resulted in a lack of coordination among governmental agencies and led to administrative chaos.

One of the most fascinating semi-autonomous agencies functioning during the Bosch period was the Inter-American Center of Social Studies (CIDES). CIDES, headed by the mysterious international operator Sacha Volman, was ostensibly a nongovernmental center for socio-economic training, but it received funds from private U.S. organizations as well as from the U.S. government and performed many additional official and unofficial services for the Bosch government. It became a brain trust, a kitchen cabinet, an educational center, a planning board, a bill-drafting organization, an administrative clearing house, and a mass education center—all in one. Because of its activities, this organization was considered by many Dominicans (and some U.S. journalists) to be a Communist apparatus. It undoubtedly performed many useful services for the Dominican government, but dissolved as soon as Bosch was overthrown. Nothing comparable to this many-faceted organization, which was often able to cut through the jungle of bureaucratic red tape both in Santo Domingo and Washington and get things done, has since then been established.

The role played and the functions performed by the Dominican public service in the post-Trujillo years were fluid, conflicting, and rapidly changing. The traditional style and pattern of bureaucratic behavior—widespread nepotism, corruption, politically determined appointments and removals, lethargy, lack of professionalism, and inefficiency—came into conflict with new pressures. Big government, the need for large numbers of technically well-trained personnel, de-Trujilloization, the organization of state employees, expanded social services, the struggle for a civil-service law, austerity programs, central planning, and the windfall of the former Trujillo properties which brought forth a whole flock of problematical autonomous and semi-autonomous government agencies—all these new developments put pressure on the bureaucracy. This conflict between old norms and new demands and pressures often resulted in strikes or threats of strike by government workers, in turmoil, disruption, instability, and in challenge to vested interests and frustration of the forces working for rapid change. These are the classic conflicts of a bureaucracy that is experiencing the transition from traditional to modern ways.

LAW AND THE LEGAL SYSTEM

Little is known about the effect of the Dominican law and legal system on the country's political processes. As in all nations, the object of Dominican law is to maintain public order and social harmony; to protect the property, moral, and individual rights of the Dominicans; and to provide for the development and progress of the country. But there have been hardly any studies of how the legal system actually works and what impact the law has in the Dominican Republic.

The Dominican Republic has a code-law legal system—that is, a system based on the Roman codification of law which was revived in Continental Europe through Justinian's Code and centuries later found expression in the Napoleonic Code. In contrast to the British or U.S. common-law systems, which are based on the principles of *stares decisis* or judicial precedent, the code-law system is a methodical and complete body of written law that covers all contingencies. Whereas custom and usage are a fundamental basis of the common law, the law remains absolute in a code system and cannot be modified or reinterpreted easily.

The code-law system in force in the Dominican Republic is French in origin. Whereas all other independent countries of Spanish America in the nineteenth century had systems derived from Spanish law, the Dominican Republic adopted the French codes because of the French-Haitian influence on the other end of the island. The law was never adapted to the realities of Dominican life and society. Indeed, it was not until some forty years after their adoption that the French codes were translated into Spanish. As Froilán Taváres, former professor of law at the University of Santo Domingo, has stated: "The conclusion we are forced to accept . . . is that a Dominican law, properly so-called, does not exist. . . . There is nothing or almost nothing that we have created; we have not elaborated nor transformed intelligently any foreign institution to adapt it to our national temperament."

The principal sections of the codes deal with civil law, such as marriage and divorce, commercial law, and criminal or penal law. Other codes have been adopted dealing with administrative law, labor law, military law, and ecclesiastical law. Practically every sector of Dominican society has its own set of laws and its own juridical basis.

The codes are logical, clearly written, and certain. They contain exact definitions and detailed specifics concerning procedures. But the impression remains that however beautifully conceived and written, the Dominican laws and legal system have little connection with the way of life of most Dominicans.

The judicial process is slow and costly. Certain corporate sectors, such as the military, receive special favors from the law. The codes are rigid and are not changed frequently enough to take care of the new social interrelationships emerging in an increasingly complex society. The labor code, for example, is badly out of date and is prejudicial against the working class.

Equity in the Anglo-American legal sense does not exist. Although individual rights are emphasized, groups or units (such as the family) and paternal power receive special recognition and are protected. The alliance between politics and law is extremely close; and excessive legalism and paper work are characteristic. The law is the law of the economic and social leaders of the country and not of the lower classes. The country's poor do not often find the legal system and the courts on their side.

Although there have been no adequate studies of the practical effects of the Dominican law and legal system on the political process, some thoughts on this matter may be tentatively offered. With its excessive emphasis on individual as opposed to public rights, the codes reinforce extreme political individualism and personalism in politics. The absolutism and certainty of the codes seem to be reflected in the highly ideological, uncompromising, and unpragmatic nature of politics in the Dominican Republic. This may also help to explain why Dominican governments try continuously to solve the nation's problems either by writing more perfect laws or by simply drafting a new constitution ("constitutional engineering"). Disputes are not settled by negotiation but by an either-or adjudication where one side—or the other—may claim to have a monopoly on truth and virtue. Reasoning tends to be deductive and based on absolute general principles, rather than inductive and scientific. Clearly, the law and legal system of the Dominican Republic tend to reinforce and perpetuate the severe divisions already existing in the country.

The governmental structures of the Dominican Republic are thus in many ways as underdeveloped and unmodern as its economy and social system. There is little tradition of constitutionalism and little basic acceptance of or consensus on the rules that govern the functioning of the political system. The political institutions that do exist are weak and fragile, and their operations often bear little correspondence to constitutional niceties.

The public service is in a state of flux, tension, and uncertainty; traditional norms and habits are being challenged, and new demands, new pressures, and new behavioral patterns are being felt. The legal system also has little to do with Dominican reality and doubtlessly contributes to the unpragmatic and unstable nature of the country's politics. In looking at the Dominican Republic's formal government structure, one finds frail, uncertain, and unstable institutions and traditions that are generally based on foreign models and have little or no basis in the Dominican experience. Gross deviations often exist between the realities of politics and government and the legal or constitutional norms. In the next chapter we shall be looking at these more informal aspects of the political process.

Chapter XI

POLITICAL PROCESSES

THE DOMINICAN REPUBLIC's governmental structure has a number of basic weaknesses that are not immediately remediable and that continue to impede the development of the country as a modern nation. When a country has a political system with little respect for and loyalty to constitutional principles, a public service torn by violently conflicting norms and behavior patterns, fragile political institutions, and a legal system that seems unrelated to the country's experience or the realities of its peoples' lives, then that country does not exhibit a high degree of political modernity. The governmental institutions and traditions of the Dominican Republic do not provide an adequate structural base for the country to deal with the profound and revolutionary changes currently taking place; and, within a democratic framework, it seems doubtful whether the present or any other administration can remedy the immense social and economic ills that plague the nation.

As the formal governmental structures are weak, uncertain, and unstable, so also the country's more informal political processes do not adequately perform their functions. The organizations—such as political parties and interest associations—which in more developed political systems serve as effective intermediaries between governed and government, as channels of demands as well as of fulfillment—are in the Dominican Republic weak, imbalanced, and ineffective. Rather than a functioning, viable system, political processes in the Dominican Republic are highly dysfunctional.

POLITICAL PARTIES

Political parties in the Dominican Republic have had a very short history. In fact, it was only after Trujillo's assassination in 1961 that a modern political party system began to emerge.

Unlike many Latin American nations, the Dominican Republic did not know the traditional, nineteenth-century liberal and conservative parties. The few political groups then were highly personalistic and usually represented rival first-family alliances with little or no differences in program or ideology. None of these groups were well organized, disciplined, or lasting, and nothing resembling a modern political party existed. Control of the government was most often determined by the political leader, usually a military *caudillo*, who could muster enough support to take power. Sumner Welles, in his history of the Dominican Republic, summarized the situation in this way: "It was a classic struggle on the part of the 'ins' to retain their power and on the part of the 'outs' to return to power. Under such conditions the twentieth century dawned in Santo Domingo without even the vestige of a tradition of constitutional government or practice."*

The fledgling political organizations that had begun to emerge in the 1920's were quickly snuffed out after Trujillo took power in 1930. The Partido Dominicano, founded one year after the dictator became president, served Trujillo for thirty years as the political apparatus to assist him in controlling the government machinery and the nation. Only incidentally did the PD perform the functions that are normally attributed to a political party. Its chief purpose was to help Trujillo maintain his dictatorial regime.

* *Naboth's Vineyard*, p. 903.

This brief historical consideration of the position of political parties in the Dominican Republic throws light upon more recent politics in the country. Traditionally there had been no genuine political parties or a party system in the Dominican Republic; and during Trujillo's rule a single party, under the absolute control of one man, dominated political life. The country had no experience with a functioning party system and its citizens had no conception of what the nature or functions of a true political party were. The Dominicans had no experience in campaigning, electing, or governing by political parties. These factors help account for the immaturity and fluidity of the party system as it evolved in the post-Trujillo years.

The present-day political-party system in the Dominican Republic began to take shape while Trujillo was still in power. Some of the many exiles banded together in Caracas, Mexico City, Havana, San José, New York, or San Juan and formed opposition groups that became the nuclei of the political parties that came into existence after Trujillo's assassination. Other anti-Trujillo groups were organized clandestinely within the Dominican Republic during the last two years of the dictator's rule; and upon his overthrow, these, too, were converted into political parties.

Foremost among the exile groups was the Dominican Revolutionary Party (PRD). The PRD was founded in 1939 by the writer and intellectual Juan Bosch, who had gone into exile a few years after Trujillo came to power. The Party's program called for the creation of a democratic political, social, and economic order in the Dominican Republic. The PRD was closely associated with other Latin American parties of the democratic left, and Bosch liked to say that it was "spiritually attuned" to the New Deal of Franklin D. Roosevelt and, later, to the New Frontier of John F. Kennedy.

For some twenty years, the PRD constituted the major exile opposition to the Trujillo regime. From its several branch offices, it put out a continuous flow of propaganda, exposing the terror and corruption of the dictatorship. After Trujillo was assassinated, the most important PRD leaders returned to the Dominican Republic and began the organizational and campaign efforts that a year and a half later would carry them to power.

The Fourteenth of June Movement (*Catorce de Junio*), another organization that later emerged as a major political party, was also formed while Trujillo was still in power. Taking its name from the invasion attempt against the Trujillo regime of June 14, 1959, and its inspiration from the martyrs of the dictator's brutal security forces, a group of Dominicans, mostly students and young people of good families, formed a clandestine movement to oppose the regime. Following the death of the Generalissimo, the *Catorcistas* converted their group into an open civic-patriotic organization and later a political party. It attracted some of the country's most prominent citizens, who pledged to work for the establishment of democracy. Only later did the Catorcistas begin to veer toward Communism.

On July 15, 1961, the formation of a third major political group, the National Civic Union (UCN), was announced. It consisted mostly of business and professional elements and was headed by Dr. Viriato Fiallo, a respected physician. The UCN was vigorously anti-Trujillo, but it was not so emphatically democratic or reform-oriented as either the PRD or the Catorce de Junio.

These three groups were influential in bringing the long Trujillo family dictatorship to an end. For the Trujillo regime, it will be recalled, did not end with the assassination of the dictator on May 30, 1961, but lingered on under Trujillo's son and heir Ramfis, who continued to jail the party leaders, break up their rallies, and raid their headquarters. Still, the opposition continued to thrive and grow. After the Trujillos and later Balaguer had been forced out of the country, elections scheduled, and a Council of State established in early 1962, political-party activity became even more in earnest, and a fledgling multiparty system began to develop.

Major changes were already taking place within the largest political parties which had led the opposition to continued Trujillo rule. Prior to the overthrow of the Trujillo regime, the UCN and the Fourteenth of June Movement, both formed as patriotic civic action associations, had worked closely together, and many prominent Dominicans were members of both groups. Now, with their common cause—the removal of the Trujillos—accomplished, an ever-widening split developed between them: the Catorce de Junio went steadily toward the left, and the UCN went steadily toward the right.

The UCN supported the establishment of the Council of State while the Fourteenth of June Movement accused it of being a reactionary and oligarchic government. The latter then accused the former of harboring *trujillistas* and of being the official party of the Council. The Catorcistas' antipathy to all U.S. activities became almost xenophobic, seeing "Yankee imperialist" plots everywhere. Their leaders' call for a revolution patterned after Castro's became more insistent. Its increasingly revolutionary and *Fidelista* stance caused many Fourteenth of June Movement members to leave the organization, and it was eventually reduced to the status of a minor party.

While the Catorcistas were increasingly leaning to the left, the UCN, though still mouthing revolutionary slogans, was going further to the right. Its moderate program was not attractive in an increasingly reform-minded society. The emergence of Bosch's PRD as a strong, left-of-center, and reformist but non-Communist party forced the UCN even more to the right on the political spectrum, and the damning epithet "party of the rich" was quickly associated with it. This three-way division among bitterly and sometimes violently opposed and irreconcilable forces—the extreme left, the center left, and the center right—has been perpetuated in the Dominican Republic to the present time.

Though the UCN, the Fourteenth of June Movement, and the PRD emerged initially as the largest political groups in the country, several minor and a number of infinitesimal "pocket" or miniparties were also formed during this period, adding further diversity to the electoral panorama. The most important of the minor groups is the Revolutionary Social Christian Party (PRSC). The PRSC is a Christian democratic party which purports to offer a Christian and "communitarian" middle way between capitalism and socialism. The PRSC often worked with Bosch's PRD. Among the other minor parties, the Dominican Revolutionary Vanguard (VRD), under Horacio Ornes, seemed to fluctuate opportunistically between left and right. The Democratic Nationalist Revolutionary Party (PNRD) was the personal apparatus of the regional *caudillo* General Miguel Angel Ramírez Alcántara. Similarly, the Social Democratic Alliance (ASD) consisted of the followers of Juan Isidro Jiménez-Grullón, a writer, intellectual, and critic of all recent Dominican governments.

Four parties existed on the extreme left—of which the Fourteenth of June Movement, pro-Castro, intensely nationalistic, and bitterly anti-U.S., was the most important. The Dominican Communist Party (PCD), formerly called the Popular Socialist Party, was the old, official Communist Party and generally adhered to a Moscow orientation. The Dominican Popular Movement (MPD), also a Communist party, is ideologically closer to the Chinese position. (Significantly, both the PCD and the MPD had at various times worked closely with Trujillo.) The Revolutionary Nationalist Party (PNR) was an exceedingly small group composed of several Marxist intellectuals. These extreme left parties, however, were not well organized, had little public support, lacked a charismatic leader like Fidel Castro, were not united, and, indeed, frequently fought among themselves or worked at cross purposes.

In addition to the major and minor parties, some twenty to twenty-five miniparties emerged during the 1962 campaign. Most were little more than paper organizations, existing one day and disappearing, merging, or further splintering the next. Some consisted only of the immediate family of the party leaders, though often a few friends and relatives would consent to have their names placed on the membership rolls. None of these small, personalistic parties figured prominently in the election campaigns or gained importance after 1962.

The wide variety of political organizations was confusing to the Dominicans, untrained in the practices of a party system. More often, allegiance went to the person of the leader rather than to his program. In 1962, the parties gave out campaign buttons, and to wear buttons from more than one party was considered both more decorative and more democratic. The ranks of total party membership came to exceed the number of eligible voters, since many Dominicans joined two or several parties. The parties and the entire party system were highly fluid and unstable and resembled what Maurice Duverger in his classic book *Political Parties** referred to as the "prehistoric era of parties":

> A country in which opinion is divided among several groups which are unstable, fluid, and short-lived does not provide an example of multi-partism in the proper sense of the term; it is still in the prehistoric era of parties; it is to be situated in that phase of general development at which the distinction between bipartism and multi-partism is not yet applicable because there are as yet no true parties.

The strongest, best-organized, and most important party was the Dominican Revolutionary Party. The PRD had headquarters in almost every community in the country, and its labor and peasant branches were also well organized. The Party used the

* London: Methuen, 1954, p. 228.

radio to reach many previously isolated potential voters and made effective use of television and the press. The PRD's program and ideology were clear, consistent, and simple, and its campaign, under the direction of Angel Miolán, was competently and professionally managed. The nature and extent of the PRD's activities clearly demonstrated that it represented considerably more than merely the personal following of Juan Bosch.

The UCN was not so well organized, ideologically consistent, or professionally run as the PRD. Furthermore, in 1962 the UCN's presidential candidate, Viriato Fiallo, was a political novice and lacked charismatic appeal. (He always wore sunglasses—even inside—which reminded many Dominicans of the Trujillos.) The UCN, nevertheless, did open offices throughout the countryside, published newspapers, and conducted a vigorous campaign. The minor parties also opened a number of regional party headquarters; but the activities of the many minor parties, including the extreme left groups, were, by and large, confined to the capital city.

As the campaign drew to a close, it became clear that the PRD and the UCN were the major competitors. But in the course of the campaign, the UCN had come to be identified with the oligarchy, with the unpopular Council of State, and with reaction. Although there are several reasons for the PRD's victory —such as its strong organization and the charisma of Bosch— the primary factor in the balloting was socio-economic class standing. Bosch's PRD became known as the party of the peasant and the worker, while Fiallo's UCN was considered the party of the rich. In a country where the poor outnumber the rich by an overwhelming majority, the PRD swept to a 2:1 victory and won comparable majorities in both houses of Congress and in local campaigns.

"What the country needs more than a good winner is good losers," said U.S. Ambassador John Bartlow Martin. But those who had lost the election were not "good losers"; the concept of a "loyal opposition" was unknown in Dominican politics, and the UCN and the other parties icily rejected President-elect Bosch's offer to join with him in a government of national unity.

Bosch was thus forced to rule without the support of any but his own party. Although the PRD had a comfortable majority in the Congress, the electoral margins did not reflect the real power configurations in the country. Eventually, the numerically weak opposition united into an anti-government coalition which, in alliance with the military, the Church, and the business elements, overthrew the Dominican Republic's first freely elected, constitutional government in thirty-eight years after it had been in office only seven months.

Following the overthrow of the Bosch administration, governmental authority was returned to the same conservative and business-oriented elements whom Bosch had beaten soundly in the election nine months before. The PRD, along with the parties of the extreme left, saw their offices closed, their leaders exiled, and their members often persecuted. The 1963 coup severely disrupted the emerging political party system and led directly to the violent revolution of 1965.

With the promise of new elections, first scheduled for 1965 and then postponed by the revolution until 1966, two new parties were formed. The Reformist Party (PR) consisted of the personal following of former President Joaquín Balaguer. Balaguer was tainted with the *trujillista* stigma, but he remained popular with some Dominicans because he had doled out part of the Trujillo wealth to the people. Also, he was generally considered to be honest, able, and moderate. The Liberal Evolutionist Party (PLE), headed by Luís Amiama Tió, one of the two survivors of the group that had assassinated Trujillo, was a rightist organization that never gained much popular following.

As in 1962, two candidates and their parties—Bosch and the PRD and Balaguer and his Reformistas—quickly emerged as the front-runners in the 1966 campaign. The National Integration

Movement (MIN) rallied several personalistic and rightist parties, including the old UCN, behind a third candidate, former President Rafael Bonnelly, but it did not attract many adherents. To most observers, the results of the election were a surprise. Balaguer beat Bosch easily, and the PR won congressional majorities equivalent to those of the PRD in 1962. Shortly after the election, the PRD was torn again by internal conflicts that seemed far more serious than the minor splits that had previously occurred within the Party.

Although the present party situation offers little cause for optimism about the emergence of a functioning and stable multiparty system in the Dominican Republic, the political parties have performed some notable functions in the short time they have been in existence. They have helped mobilize, educate, and bring into politics previously isolated sectors of the population. They have begun to serve as channels of communication between rulers and ruled and have, in the few years since the end of Trujillo's perverted single-party system, become an integral part of the Dominican political process.

Yet, the Dominican parties are not by any means adequately performing all the functions demanded in a more modern, democratic system. Even the major parties—such as Balaguer's Reformist Party—are highly personalistic and weakly organized. Some would argue that in the Dominican political system personalities such as Bosch, Fiallo, Jiménez-Grullón, and Balaguer are still far more important than the impersonal *partidos*. The existence of so many parties with such extremely varied orientations also tends to reinforce and perpetuate the deep divisions that already exist in the Dominican society. With the possible exception of the PRD, the parties perform only a limited role in educating the people in democratic procedures, in bringing together diverse interests, in selecting leaders, in communicating popular demands to the government, in helping to translate these demands into actual policies, and in administering programs. There is no tradition of a conciliatory majority or of a "loyal opposition." (Again, the PRD, which proclaimed itself in "loyal, democratic, and constructive opposition" to the Balaguer government, is an exception.) The rule of one party or of an alliance of parties has historically tended to be unacceptable to the "outs," who have often found it necessary to subvert or overthrow the government in power, while the "ins" have usually ignored the wishes of—and sometimes have even persecuted—those not in power. Under these conditions, the prospects for a stable and viable political party system, in which the parties perform adequately the minimum functions required in a more modern and more democratic political system, are not bright.

INTEREST ORGANIZATIONS

A wide variety of free, independent, and competitive interest organizations are essential in a modern democratic system. Indeed, democracy may be defined as a system in which as many groups as possible participate in the political process and in which all major interests are fairly evenly represented in the decision-making of the government. Interest associations help to mobilize and educate the people, give them an organized voice in political affairs, and serve as links between individuals, parties, and the government. A major guarantee against dictatorships such as Trujillo's and for the emergence of a pluralistic democratic system is the existence of a large number of interest organizations that are truly competitive and balanced enough to prevent a single interest, or an alliance of a few interests, from dominating the country. Modern democratic systems thus require not only an institutional network of checks and balances (for example, between executive and legislature), but also a network of social and economic checks and balances (for example, between labor and business).

The Dominican Republic does not have a wide variety of interest organizations competing in the political process. The relatively few organized interests are not very effective in performing the mobilization, education, organization, or linkage functions. Furthermore, the several interest associations are not truly competitive, and certain groups—primarily the military and the business, professional, and landowning elite—have overwhelming power. The Dominican Republic is not a country in which political, social, or governmental checks and balances operate effectively; rather, it is a political system which is highly imbalanced and in which the few, not the many, rule.

The Military

The armed forces are perhaps the most powerful domestic interest organization in Dominican politics. Historically, the military has been far more influential as a maker and unmaker of governments than as the nation's defender. Its war and defense potential is limited, but as a shaper and determiner of internal political affairs, it is a most important force. Only at their own peril can Dominican governments disregard the interests of the armed forces; indeed, before enacting any policy, the prudent Dominican president will first consider how the military, then how the business, professional, and landowning elite, and then how other groups in descending order of importance will react. The principle of civilian control over the armed forces has never been fully accepted. For example, President Donald Reid's assumption of the post of Minister of the Armed Forces, a position jealously reserved by the military for one of its generals, was a major factor in the overthrow of his government.

While the military has frequently meddled in politics and has, at times, overthrown civil and constitutional governments, in all fairness it should be recognized that civilian meddling in the armed forces occurs just as frequently. Recognizing the immense political power of the military, many civilian politicians attempt to organize their own personal cliques within the officer corps. (The pro-Balaguer group of officers, for example, is known as the "San Cristóbal Crowd.") From the armed forces' point of view, military involvement in politics is justified by the politicians' interference in military affairs and by what the armed forces conceive to be threats to their existence or their professional and institutional place in society.

The Dominican military, however, is often motivated to interfere in politics for other, less justifiable reasons. Corruption is rampant within the military, and some officers become involved in political coups—such as those against Bosch and Reid—if only to preserve the means of their illegal enrichment. The armed forces are still conditioned by the oppressive habits and practices learned during the Trujillo era. Many of the officers tend to see the specter of "Communism" in all reform proposals and have remained adamantly opposed to Bosch, his party, and allied groups because they feared that these democratic left-wing elements would convert the Dominican Republic into a "second Cuba" (which, of course, implies the destruction of the regular armed forces and the shooting of many of its officers). Personal as well as institutional self-interest—and not so much considerations of the national interest—are what prompts the military to intervene in politics.

Attempts have been made in recent years to reform the Dominican military and to involve it in constructive civic action programs rather than in corrupt and oppressive practices. Despite elaborate efforts to retrain, reorient, and reorganize the military, however, few roads or schools have been built, and the full professionalization of the armed forces remains a distant goal.

Almost all Dominicans wish to retain their armed forces, if for no other reason than that a strong military is a symbol of nationhood and of national power and sovereignty. But many Dominicans question whether the military sector should continue to enjoy such a privileged place in society. The comparatively huge armed forces—10,000 in the National Police (there are no local or provincial police), 3,000 in the Navy, 4,000 in the Air Force, and 12,000 in the Army—drain off some 40 per cent of the national budget, funds that could be spent more profitably on education and on development projects.

The Dominican military is not a monolithic force opposed to all democratic reforms. Although, at times, rivalries exist between the services (the Air Force and Navy are commonly considered more respectable than the Army and the Police), divisions occur more often between the older and younger officers. Many of the younger officers are appalled by the corruption in the upper ranks and share the belief that the armed forces should be professionalized, apolitical, and dedicated to constructive civic action programs. (To many Dominicans, the 1965 intervention of U.S. military forces in their country represented U.S. support for the small group of *trujillista* generals in command and opposition to the more democratically inclined younger officers.)

The Dominican armed forces remain the strongest force in national politics—with veto power over almost all major government policies. The huge military cannot be wished away; it is a force with which political leaders must deal realistically, if their programs are to succeed and their governments to survive. It will require considerable time before the armed forces are conditioned not to use this immense power to crush the weaker sectors of the society and to prevent democratic social and political development.

The Business, Professional, and Landowning Elite

The business, professional, and landowning elite has neither the arms nor the strong organization of the military, but it is nevertheless a powerful political force. The power of the elite stems from its wealth and its intricate and extensive system of family, business, and government connections. On a day-to-day basis, the elite is probably an even more important force than the military.

Formal organization is less important to the wealthy elite than to the armed forces. Its organizations include the Chamber of Commerce, Agriculture, and Industry; the Association of Industries; the Association of Landowners and Agriculturists; and the Patronal Association. Some of the professional associations often work in alliance with business, agricultural, and industrial associations. Politically, the wealthier elements grouped together after Trujillo's death in the UCN, but as we have seen this party disintegrated almost completely after losing the 1962 elections. The elite often prefers to work through temporary *ad hoc* organizations. Independent Dominican Action (ADI), was one of the more prominent of these, forming in 1963 to lead the opposition against the Bosch government. Since the elite has so far been able to protect its interests through other means, it has not seen the need to create a permanent, modern, mass-based political party.

As was the case with regard to the military, the elite is not a monolithic oligarchy wholly opposed to change. Some business leaders, particularly the progressive-minded group in the Santiago Development Association, are interested in stimulating reform and modernization. A few of the wealthier elements worked closely with the Bosch government in 1963 and were sympathetic to the constitutionalist cause in the 1965 revolution. But, while some elite elements—particularly the "old rich" oligarchs whose social position is secure—are progressive or feel a sense of *noblesse oblige*, many of the Dominican Republic's wealthier elements—especially the "new rich" businessmen in the capital—remain steadfastly opposed to any social-democratic reforms. The latter seem to be more numerous than is actually the case because they are more activist and more vocal than the former.

The elite community does not appear to be very well organized or disciplined. Their associations are only loosely organized, and few members bother to attend meetings. On most minor issues, only the presidents of the associations are likely to speak out. But on major issues—such as the Bosch government, which the business-commercial group considered a threat to its long-held privileged position—the elite can be quickly mobilized. Petty differences are put aside, and the oligarchy will usually act clannishly as a single unit—powerful and almost invincible. Because the elite is a small, intimate group in which all know each other or are interrelated, there is little need for a tightly knit organization; the telephone and personal contacts serve equally well.

The concerted power of this element in Dominican politics is enormous. A popular mandate by ballot may be meaningless since, between elections, only a few wealthy and prestigious families actually rule the country. Many Dominicans feel that if the oligarchy refuses to respond to the need for peaceful and democratic reforms, the only alternative may be a Castro-like revolution. If the elite elements refuse to sacrifice some of their wealth and prerogatives in a slow and orderly fashion, a violent revolution may force them one day to give up everything. Thus far, there is little evidence that such reasoning has impressed more than a few of the wealthier business elements or that they have become more reform and democratically oriented.

The Church

The Catholic Church, as a human institution, also functions as a strong interest organization in the Dominican Republic. The nature of religious sentiment, the organization and structure of the Church, and the divisions and crosscurrents within its ranks have been discussed in Chapter VI; but we might profitably discuss at this point how the Church makes its influence felt in the political realm.

As an interest organization, the Church influences politics in a number of ways. At times of grave crises, the hierarchy may issue a pastoral letter to be read from all pulpits and printed in the major newspapers. The Church may also make its voice heard over its own radio stations and through special programs on other stations. A few clerics hold positions in the government, and others write regularly in the daily press on moral and social questions. Often, high-ranking Church officials are present at important government functions. In some towns, the local priest may be the best educated and most influential member of the community, so that on a day-to-day basis little is done without his approval or acquiescence.

The Church's influence may also be measured by its role in a variety of social services. As of 1963, some 900 nuns and numerous trainees were in the Dominican Republic, many of them serving as teachers, nurses, or social workers. The Church itself runs thirty-seven schools, seven hospitals, and an unknown number of relief stations, social centers, and cooperatives. Through Caritas, it distributes food to thousands of hungry Dominicans. Priests serve as chaplains in public schools and hospitals and in the armed forces. Through these and other extensive social services and activities, the Church inevitably exercises political influence.

The Church may also exert pressure through several lay organizations and nonconfessional political and labor groups that derive their inspiration from Catholic principles. Lay groups such as Catholic Action, the Legion of Merit, the Apostles of Prayer, and the Marianos are active; but none of them plays a significant political role. More important are the Revolutionary Social Christian Party (PRSC) and the Autonomous Confederation of Christian Syndicates (CASC). Although the PRSC and the CASC are not formally linked to the Church, and although their political perspectives are often at wide variance from those of the hierarchy, both look to the Church for their principles and are often connected with it by informal ties.

Despite this wide range of activities, the Church's political influence in the Dominican Republic is probably not so important as that of the military or the business-professional-landowning elite, and it is less important than that of the Church in other Latin American countries. Although the power of its moral pressure is considerable, the Church is not, as was the case with the military and the elite, a veto group. It cannot expect to see its dictates entirely accepted in the political arena, nor can it impose its wishes on an uncooperative government. As we have seen, the Church's political power is decisive only if it can join with other influential sectors of the population. Such was the case with regard to the government of Juan Bosch. As an individual interest organization, the Church could do little except express its opposition to Bosch and his policies. But when the spiritual power of the Church was united with the military might of the Dominican armed forces and the economic power of the oligarchy, Bosch's government quickly fell.

In response to the reaction against the obstructionist and negative image that the Church had acquired, and which came to light again as intense anti-Church sentiment during the 1965 revolution, the Church has begun to play a more positive and constructive role in social and political affairs. Not only did the Church begin to take a more active part in promoting social justice, encouraging education, working with the poor, and pushing reforms, but it also, led by the Papal Nuncio, Emmanuel Clarizzio, began to serve as a positive force in bringing together and possibly reconciling the contending Dominican factions. Whether the Church can recoup some of its lost moral and political influence remains to be seen.

The Middle Sectors

A variety of organized interest associations exists that speak for one or another element of the middle sectors. These include the Rotary Club, which issues occasional statements about the national economy; the Association of Lawyers; the Association of Engineers and Architects; and others with more openly political interests. But, unlike the interest associations previously considered, these organizations of the middle sectors do not often speak with a single voice. As discussed in Chapter VII, the Dominican middle groups have little sense of class-consciousness, and they are in fact highly divided about the goals for the society and the means to achieve them. Indeed, much of the conflict within the Dominican political arena is a reflection of the divisions that exist between the different elements of the middle sectors.

Nevertheless, the middle sectors are increasing in size and influence. The professionals, business groups, government workers, and so forth who make up the ranks of the growing middle groups are playing an increasingly important role in politics, government, communications, and the economy. But because they are so deeply divided in outlook and ideology, their impact on politics is still weak, particularly in comparison with that of the armed forces and the business-professional-landowning elite.

Organized Labor

Organized labor in developing countries is often comparable in importance to political parties as a means by which a large sector of the population that has previously not been integrated into the political and social life of the country may make its influence felt in national decision-making. Unions are therefore an essential ingredient for the development of a modern, pluralistic, and democratic political system.

What makes labor so important in the modernization process is that its activities are not confined to the economic sphere but spill over into the political realm as well. Political activity, such as general strikes, demonstrations, and violence, is often a more effective—and sometimes the only—method for labor to get what it wants. In this context, collective bargaining is not appropriate or useful. Labor movements in developing countries such as the Dominican Republic are out of necessity intrinsically bound to political movements, since the gap between workers and employers is usually too wide to be peacefully bridged at the bargaining table. Labor tends to be highly ideological, its demands radical, and its role revolutionary. As a political force, then, the labor organizations take on added importance in the process of development.

Prior to 1930, there was no organized labor movement to speak of in the Dominican Republic. And during the Trujillo era, the emerging trade-union movement was tightly controlled by the dictatorship. Only after Trujillo was slain did labor begin to develop organized and politically important units. This development was neither smooth, peaceful, nor totally successful. The movement was frequently torn by disagreements and violent conflict, and the federations fought as often among themselves as with their natural opponents, the employers and the *patrones*. Unions frequently transferred their allegiance from one federation to another and the workers from one union to another. Although the labor movement is still in its infancy, its importance should not be underestimated.

Out of the initial turmoil and divisionism of 1961–62, a number of major and minor labor organizations developed. The National Confederation of Free Workers (CONATRAL) performed some notable recruiting, educational, and organizational services; but it often functioned as the labor arm of the U.S. government and was thus discredited in the eyes of many Dominicans. The Pro-Independent Labor Unions Front–Central Syndicate of Dominican Workers (FOUPSA-CESITRADO) was closely linked with the PRD, while the Autonomous Confederation of Christian Syndicates (CASC) was the labor branch of the Revolutionary Social Christian Party.

The National Federation of Teachers (FENAMA) and the National Federation of Public Employees and Employees of Autonomous Agencies (FENEPIA) were smaller but nevertheless politically important because of the people they spoke for, and because they were often allied with the extreme left. The Communists were organized under a variety of names but did not gain a strong foothold in the labor movement. A number of important unions—the cement workers, the brewery workers, the rum workers employed by Bermúdez, the tobacco workers, the telephone workers, the electrical workers, and the sugar (Rio Haina) workers—were not affiliated with any of the major confederations.

In terms of recruitment and organization, significant gains were made. Some 500 unions with a total membership of close to 200,000 had been organized by the end of 1966. The new labor organizations achieved wage increases, often in excess of 100 per cent, and other increased benefits for the workers. This was a very different situation from that of the Trujillo era when, with no effective or independent organization to represent them, the workers were virtual serfs.

While much has been accomplished in the labor movement in a short span of time, many problems persist. One of these is the lack of trained and experienced union leaders. Another is the poverty of the workers, who cannot afford the dues necessary so that their unions may carry on day-to-day activities. Suspicion of unions still exists on the part of the workers and hostility toward them on the part of the employers, who invent numerous schemes, including favors to spurious Communist unions, to confuse and further divide labor.

The major problem, however, remains labor's comparatively

weak political position as a force for democratic development and modernization. The individual unions are loosely organized, the federations are really *con*federations among which the individual unions frequently shift affiliations, and the several federations do not speak with a united voice for all labor. This difficulty is well illustrated at the giant La Romana sugar complex where thirty-one unions—six affiliated with CONATRAL, seven with FOUPSA-CESITRADO, and eighteen independents —frequently work at cross purposes, both with the management and with each other. Furthermore, the close identification of the federations with political parties has weakened labor in general and has served to reinforce and perpetuate the deep ideological cleavages that already divided Dominican society. The labor movement in the Dominican Republic emerged as a significant interest association in the period after Trujillo, but in comparison with other organized elements—such as the military or the elite—it remains fluid, highly fragmented, and politically weak.

The Peasantry

The Dominican peasantry is numerically the largest but politically and organizationally the weakest of the country's social sectors. The *campesinos* have traditionally been neglected and ignored and have not been brought in as full participant members of the national system. Because the *campesinos* have never had an effective organized voice, they have always been isolated and atomized, unable to communicate their wants and demands to the government, and without any means to exert pressure to promote or protect their interests. Although this situation has begun to change in the post-Trujillo years, it has not changed very rapidly, and the peasant is still the forgotten man of Dominican politics.

When honest and fair elections are held, as in 1962 and 1966, the peasants' vote counts as much as that of other Dominicans, but during the interval between elections, only a very few people exercise power, and the *campesinos* are once again forgotten. The political parties managed to bring out the peasant vote in 1962 and 1966, but little in the way of a permanent organization for the peasantry was continued after the elections. The PRD's peasant arm—the National Federation of Peasant Brotherhoods (FENHERCA)—was the largest peasant association ever formed in the country, but this attempt at mass mobilization of the rural population dissolved after the Bosch government fell. The Christian-democratic Dominican Federation of Peasant Leagues (FEDELAC), linked closely to the PRSC and the CASC, is currently the most effective peasant organization; but its activities have made only a minor dent in a major problem.

Other rather sporadic and uncertain efforts have been made to provide the countryside with at least a minimum organizational structure. The several governments' agrarian reform and cooperative programs were oriented in this direction; but these efforts have not been very successful. Peace Corps volunteers, private groups, development foundations, the Dominican Office of Community Development, and U.S. aid officials have also been active in rural areas. But it will require much more time, energy, and expense before the Dominican *campesinos* will be able to bargain collectively and effectively in the political process. For the most part, the peasants remain isolated from national affairs and have almost no say in the making of decisions that most intimately affect them.

The entire Dominican political process seems to be dysfunctional. Thus, the country's political parties are not adequately performing the functions of political education, leadership selection, presentation of alternative programs, harmonization of diverse and conflicting interests, political aggregation, and communication. Nor are the interest organizations performing satisfactorily the functions of political socialization, mobilization, organization, and interest articulation. The numerically largest sectors of the population are weak and ineffective, while a small number of wealthy, socially prominent, or militarily powerful interest groups dominate the national life. Indeed, the Dominican Republic is not a country in which the different organized interests check and balance each other—the essence of a pluralistic and democratic system—but a country with a highly imbalanced system in which, despite democratic and constitutional trappings, only a few control the society, the economy, the polity, the military forces, and the religious and belief system. The vast mass of the population has almost no influence at all. As the entire system becomes more complex, this pattern is changing—and changing at an accelerated speed—but the highly imbalanced and dysfunctional nature of the political process serves as a further impediment to rapid modernization and democratic development.

Chapter XII

PUBLIC POLICY AND FOREIGN AFFAIRS

PREVIOUS CHAPTERS have stressed the dysfunctional nature of Dominican political processes and the weaknesses of the country's governmental institutions. This chapter will discuss public policy and governmental decisions, often also referred to as the "output" of the political system. For not only are Dominican governmental institutions not wholly appropriate for the society and the political parties and interest associations performing their functions inadequately, but also the government's policies and programs are not very effective. Elaborate reform plans are often conceived, drawn up, and put into operation; but most often these programs are frustrated or have no impact at all on the people who are supposed to benefit from them. In domestic and in foreign affairs, the Dominican Republic is plagued by a host of problems that seem almost to defy solution.

PUBLIC POLICY

We have already discussed the inadequacies and ineffectiveness of governmental policies designed to spur industrialization, to deal with the armed forces, to introduce austerity programs, and, in general, to build viable democratic institutions on the ruins left by the fallen Trujillo dictatorship. The difficulties of public policy formulation and execution may, however, be best highlighted by examining in detail a single program: agrarian reform. The agrarian reform program not only vividly illustrates the problems and frustrations involved in all areas of public policy but has been considered by successive Dominican governments as one of the major keys—if not *the* key—to the development of a more efficient and diversified economy, of a more just society, and of a more democratic political system.

The enactment and successful execution of an agrarian reform program was thought to be essential for a number of reasons. The wave of democratic sentiment that swept the country after the overthrow of the Trujillo regime led many Dominicans to feel that it was no longer appropriate for a few large landowners to so completely dominate the country's agricultural wealth and effectively control the economic, social, and political destinies of the laborers or tenants working on their estates. Under the prevailing system, in which *latifundia* and *minifundia* existed side by side, much land was wasted, technical advances were slow, and the market for the goods of a society wishing to industrialize remained extremely small. Furthermore, the migration of landless peasants to the city created pressing social problems and led to a shortage of rural labor, thereby helping to undermine agricultural production.

A program had to be devised, therefore, that made the rural areas attractive enough so that the *compesinos* could be induced to remain on the land. It was felt that landownership—plus education, the formation of cooperatives and credit unions, the introduction of more efficient and profitable farming techniques, in short, a broad and integrated agrarian reform program—would provide such an incentive. It would also give a stronger political voice to the *campesino*, the Dominican Republic's traditionally forgotten man. Especially during the Bosch administration, agrarian reform was thus seen as a way to mobilize and organize the peasantry and to rally political support.

Agrarian reform programs had been carried out before in Dominican history, but only in distorted form. Trujillo, it will be recalled, confiscated much of the best land in the country, moved the dispossessed peasants to the rocky hillsides, and propagandistically labelled this "agrarian reform." Both Ramfis Trujillo and President Balaguer had engaged in grandiose land giveaways, but these gestures could hardly be called agrarian reform.

Balaguer had been replaced, in mid-January, 1962, by the caretaker Council of State, and the vast lands belonging to the Trujillos were then kept in the possession of the government. This was a golden opportunity for the Dominican Republic to launch a successful agrarian reform. Since large landholdings were already under state ownership, the government would not have to expropriate further private properties and in the process run the risk of antagonizing the Dominican *hacendados* or scaring away private foreign investment. All the government had to do was to divide efficiently the land it already possessed. Surveys revealed that there was enough state-owned land to carry out an effective agrarian reform for at least four years. Only later would the troublesome question of expropriation or confiscation of private lands have to be considered. The prospect for a successful agrarian reform seemed simple and certain.

The idea of agrarian reform was put aside early in 1962 until the Council of State had more securely established itself as a government. Then, as a first step, the Council established the Dominican Agrarian Institute in April, 1962. The Institute was charged with the responsibility for carrying out a nationwide agrarian reform program and was set up as an autonomous agency, authorized to contract its own financial obligations. The Institute was governed by a seven-man board of directors composed of the ministers of agriculture and labor, the general manager of the Agrarian Bank, and four other members chosen by the Council. Manuel de Jesús Viñas Cáceres was named director-general of the Institute, and late in May he began to organize the program.

Independent of the Agrarian Institute, however, the Council of State had already begun to distribute land to the *campesinos*. Some fifty families were given land near the city of Bonao—land that had formerly belonged to Arismendi Trujillo, a brother of the late dictator. No adequate plans had been formulated as yet for agrarian reform, however, and though the Council was no doubt motivated by a desire to make a quick and dramatic gesture to gain popular support, this land giveaway was premature and led to administrative confusion.

The Agrarian Institute, in the meantime, was still only getting organized. A contract was signed with International Development Services Inc. to provide technical assistance. Financial aid and additional technicians were also provided by a number of international agencies and foreign governments. The administrative machinery for an effective agrarian reform was also put into operation: the Agrarian Bank was to provide long-term credit to farmers; the Housing Institute was to supervise low-cost housing for the peasants; the Agrarian Institute was to distribute the land and work for a more efficient land use; and the newly created National Planning Board was to oversee the entire operation.

With the administrative machinery, the money, the technicians, and the plans ready, the Council began a more extensive land reform effort. In August, 1962, some four hundred families were settled on another former Trujillo estate. Along with the distribution of land, the government began a cooperative program to assist the peasants in the sale of their products, sent out a number of agronomy experts to find newer and better uses for the land, and started a home construction program.

After this ambitious beginning, however, the agrarian-reform program slowed down and then stopped altogether. The great public pressure to initiate an agrarian reform immediately had resulted in a hasty crash program that was flawed by a number of unsound practices. Projects to develop the nation's river system as part of the over-all plan to improve rural conditions also floundered. In addition, problems associated with the forthcoming elections forced the Council to devote more time to electoral matters and less to agrarian reform. Finally, the Council determined to defer implementation of the program since it felt that such an important issue as agrarian reform should be dealt with by an elected government.

While an auspicious start was made by the Council, little in the way of actual agrarian reform was accomplished. Only eight projects, involving a total of some 800 new landowners (only one-third of the stated goal), were initiated, and even this limited program was far from being an overwhelming success. None of the excitement and fervor that one would expect to accompany the first steps toward an agrarian social revolution was felt by the government officials who administered the program or by the peasants who received the land. The lack of enthusiasm may be partly explained by the conservative and aristocratic nature of the Council government, whose members had little interest in more than a token agrarian reform, and it is not too surprising that the Council's program failed to evoke much popular response.

The Bosch government was determined to change this. The new President's party was, after all, a popularly-based party that had swept to victory largely on the basis of its *campesino* support; also, Bosch himself was dedicated to raising the standard of living of the rural masses. In a speech shortly after his inauguration, Bosch announced that agrarian reform would be the cornerstone on which his government would rise or fall. "Agrarian reform," he said, "*is* the Dominican revolution."

Bosch replaced Viñas Cáceres with Gustavo Machado Báez

as director-general of the Agrarian Institute. Machado Báez proceeded to reorganize completely the structure of the Institute, thus causing much disruption of the Institute's regular procedures. Then Bosch appointed the Costa Rican agriculturalist Carlos Campos as his personal representative in the Institute and gave him more authority than the director-general. This effectively undermined the authority and prestige of Machado Báez and created rival jurisdictions and a sharp division of authority in the agency between the two competing leaders and their followers. In turn, these factors contributed to the confusion and lack of progress that characterized Bosch's agrarian reform program.

Another organizational change instituted by the Bosch government was the creation of a presidential coordinating committee to oversee and coordinate all the diverse governmental agencies dealing with agrarian reform. While the intention was laudable, the result was again disastrous. Responsibility for planning and carrying out the agrarian reform was taken from the Agrarian Institute and given to the fifteen-member committee. Each committee member had a different conception of agrarian reform, and the "coordinating" group worked more often at cross purposes than as a team. The system was unwieldy and inaction-by-committee resulted.

Administrative and organizational confusion soon multiplied. Another disruptive force was the PRD's peasant branch, FENHERCA, which sought to gain control over the agrarian reform program. FENHERCA's plan was to gain peasant support for the party (and itself) by the immediate redistribution of all the land under government control. However, such a program of rapid and indiscriminate land subdivision would have surely produced chaos. Furthermore, Sacha Volman, head of the Inter-American Center for Social Studies (CIDES) and Bosch's *confidant*, exercised great influence in the agrarian reform program, and this further complicated the situation.

There were other overlapping, competing, and conflicting jurisdictions as well. Carlos Campos, Bosch's personal representative in the Agrarian Institute, also worked for CIDES; and Angel Miolán, the president of the PRD, felt that he should have a say in the affairs of the peasants whom he had helped to organize. FENHERCA, in turn, received funds and technical assistance from CIDES. A variety of other agencies—including the Peace Corps, the Ministry of Public Works, the Office of Natural Resources, and the Agricultural Extension Service— had also been mobilized for the great effort. Although Bosch attempted to manage and juggle the growing number of individuals and organizations involved in the agrarian reform program, he ultimately failed. The over-all result was chaos.

The initial attempt at agrarian reform in the Bosch administration was made in mid-May, 1963, when forty families were given title to land that belonged to the government. During the next two months, while the Agrarian Institute was gathering socio-economic data on applicant families, running orientation sessions for its own employees, disseminating propaganda at the farm level, and reorganizing itself, no new titles were given to the land-hungry peasants. By failing to move quickly and dramatically, Bosch lost much of his initial *campesino* support.

Administrative difficulties were the major cause of frustration in the agrarian reform program during this period, but other factors were also involved. Many landowners who had been dispossessed by Trujillo flocked to the courts seeking title to their former land—that is, land which the government intended to use for agrarian reform. Since the Dominican judicial process is slow, much time was lost in the complicated litigation. Another problem stemmed from the mass take-over of private lands by the *campesinos*, who were reportedly acting with the approval of the PRD's peasant apparatus, FENHERCA. Claiming that the land was rightfully theirs and impatient with the slowness of the government program, thousands of peasants took the agrarian reform law into their own hands. These activities frightened the landowners and intensified their antipathy to the entire program.

During August and September, 1963, shortly before Bosch was overthrown, a concerted program finally got under way, and some six hundred families were settled in agrarian reform projects. In retrospect, however, it is especially significant that the peasant-oriented Bosch government gave out 25 per cent *less* titles to land to the *campesinos* than the preceding business-oriented Council of State government had. Bosch's accomplishments were a far cry from his goal of resettling 5,500 peasant families on 90,000 acres of former Trujillo land by the end of 1963; 25,000 families on half a million acres by 1967; and 70,000 families on the nearly one million acres of former Trujillo property by 1970.*

After Bosch's ouster, the agrarian reform program came to a halt. The conservative, business-oriented Triumvirate was beset by what it considered more crucial issues and was not primarily interested in a program that would strengthen the *campesino* sector. The entire organizational apparatus was once again completely revamped. Impressive statistics attest to the amount of land given out during Donald Reid's tenure as president, but Reid's purposes were almost exclusively political, that is, he wanted to promote support for his illegitimate and unpopular government, and his well-publicized agrarian reform consisted chiefly in handing out worthless land titles. Whatever agrarian reform existed during the Reid era ceased with the 1965 revolution. It has only been in most recent years, under Balaguer, that the agrarian reform program has been revived.

* The Bosch Government also gave permission to some 800 peasant families to remain on the land they had occupied following the Trujillos' ouster. Although these "squatter" peasants were to participate in the agrarian reform program, it would not be accurate to include them in the total number of families settled by the government.

Despite some concerted efforts, then, the agrarian reform program conducted in the Dominican Republic in the post-Trujillo years has only begun to scratch the surface of some vast, underlying problems. After half a decade of attempting to implement an agrarian reform program, the Dominican countryside remains impoverished, inefficient, and unmechanized, and the *campesinos* illiterate, ill-fed, ill-housed, ill-clothed, unorganized, landless, and still without the hope that a better life might be possible.

In the last analysis, the extremely limited success of the agrarian reform program was due to a number of factors:

1. During the short period of genuine agrarian reform since mid-1962, the program was under the direction of a succession of extremely short-lived governments. Each administration had its own idea about what constituted an effective agrarian reform, with the result that each change in government brought a complete change in the organization and orientation of the program. Political instability meant that much time, effort, and personnel were wasted during the transition from one government to another. Technicians connected with the Agrarian Institute have estimated that, because of the constant change-overs, only about half of the Institute's time was used for actual agrarian reform work.

2. Agrarian reform is both a highly technical and a highly political undertaking, and the unhappy mixture of the two in the Dominican case led to confusion, inefficiency, misunderstanding and, eventually, failure. Some aspects of the agrarian reform—such as crop improvement, the use of fertilizer, or breeding—are properly the realm of technical experts. Other facets of the program—the establishment of cooperatives and credit unions, the education, mobilization, and organization of the peasants—inevitably enter the realm of politics. Given their different concepts of agrarian reform, the technicians and the *políticos* often came in conflict. It is probably impossible to

separate the technical from the political aspects entirely, but a happier balance could have been achieved.

3. The various offices, ministries, international agencies, institutes, political organizations, and individuals involved in agrarian reform frequently disagreed, and the lack of coordination among them contributed to making a quagmire of conflicting jurisdictions and wasteful rivalries.

4. Many of the agrarian reform projects were not well planned and their objectives not clearly thought out. Some projects were hastily and erratically initiated without feasibility projections. This, in turn, caused a loss of time, money, and prestige for the Agrarian Institute and for the entire agrarian reform program. In some cases, the government gave out land without having a clear title to it, and the result was that no peasant family could be certain that it would not be evicted at some future date. The Agrarian Institute wasted much effort on preliminary studies, land surveys, and land preparation in projects that later had to be indefinitely postponed or abandoned altogether because, in some hurriedly conceived plan, nobody had bothered to clarify the land titles.

5. Some governments were simply more concerned with agrarian reform than others. Despite the malfunctioning of Bosch's agrarian reform, it was clear that during his short tenure the peasants had a friend in the National Palace, and that the government was genuinely, even passionately, interested in improving their lot. At other times, however, agrarian reform was only *pro forma*—neither the Council of State nor the Triumvirate were interested in vigorously pushing a program that was bound to erode the socio-economic order on which their power rested, and at best their land distribution efforts were halfhearted.

In its broadest sense, the agrarian reform program clearly illustrates the problems and difficulties of public policy implementation in the Dominican Republic. Elaborate plans and preparations were frequently devised, but the actual operations and the way the program was carried out was a different matter. Not only was the agrarian reform inadequate and inefficient, for all the reasons listed above, but it had almost no effect on those who were supposed to be its prime beneficiaries: the peasants themselves.

The difficulties of public policy formulation and especially of policy execution in the realm of agrarian reform are duplicated in many other policy areas—housing, health, social security, education, hydraulic resources development, and so on. There are dozens of major reform programs which successive Domini- can governments have attempted to implement but without great success. The histories of these programs are similar to that of agrarian reform—they begin as great and glorious visions and end as inglorious failures or with only minimal gains. It is not surprising that in a political system where governmental programs, despite enormous efforts, are almost wholly ineffec- tive, the entire system should be shaky and prone to breakdowns.

FOREIGN AFFAIRS

Countries such as Great Britain and the United States were able to develop, early and in relative isolation, viable democratic systems that proved to be adaptable to the stresses and strains of industrialization and of a shrinking and increasingly inter- dependent and complex, modern world. For countries like the Dominican Republic, however, which have only recently begun the drive toward modernization, these problems piled up all at once: not only did the disruptive pressures resulting from the clamor for immediate democratization come at precisely the same time as the various discontinuities accompanying the early stages of industrialization, but they occurred also at a point in history when the Cold War and increased international inter- dependence made it inconceivable that a nation could develop autonomously and without foreign interference. The Dominican Republic's foreign affairs are thus intimately tied to the country's modernization process.

The relations between the Dominican Republic and the United States are by far the most important. U.S. influence in the Dominican Republic over a long period of time, and particularly since 1959, coinciding with the coming to power of Castro and the Communists in neighboring Cuba, has been enormous. Although the word "satellite" has emotional connotations which may properly be avoided, U.S. involvement in the Dominican Republic in recent years has been so extensive that the question may be raised of just how extensive Dominican sovereignty over its own affairs is. At times, it is difficult to determine whether the U.S. Embassy or Dominican officials are actually formulating the policies and making the decisions. Even when decisions are made by Dominican authorities, however, they may well consider first the potential reactions of the United States.

U.S. influence reaches into almost all spheres of Dominican life. Since there are so many, it would be impossible to chronicle all the activities, organizations, and influences of the United States in Dominican affairs, but brief mention of some of these may provide an idea of their vast range.

Although the holdings of private American concerns are not nearly so extensive, say, as they were in Cuba prior to Castro, such companies as Esso, Texaco, Alcoa, or the South Puerto Rican Sugar Company exercise a considerable influence in Dominican domestic affairs. Furthermore, since the Dominican economy is so closely tied to the United States, this also makes the Dominican Republic subject to a variety of U.S. pressures.

In the military realm, the United States is largely responsible for the training, equipping, arming, clothing, and instructing of the Dominican armed forces. U.S. military attachés and a large military-assistance team attempt to keep a close watch on the Dominican armed forces.

Huge amounts of U.S. money, men, and materials have also been poured into the Dominican labor movement. Additionally the Peace Corps contingent in the Dominican Republic is comparatively large for a country so small. The United States Information Service (USIS) is most active in the intellectual, cultural, and communications field. CARE and Caritas feed many Dominicans through the U.S. food surplus program. Furthermore, the Agency for International Development, we should be reminded, has provided more per capita aid to the Dominican Republic than to any other Latin American country. There is an endless number of semi-private foundations, organizations, and individuals that have been active in the Dominican Republic: from the AFL-CIO to the Business Council for World Understanding; from the Ford Foundation to a variety of cover agencies for the Central Intelligence Agency; from the Farmers' Union to the American Legion Auxiliary; from former Vice-President Henry Wallace, who rolled up his sleeves and sought to improve Dominican agriculture, to a legion of international operators, influence peddlers, and super-salesmen, such as the private American entrepreneur who tried to sell the Dominican government a supply of used voting machines from upstate New York. Beginning in 1962, indeed, there were so many U.S. officials in the country that a housing shortage developed. It is virtually impossible to think of a field of endeavor in which the U.S. is not active in Dominican affairs.

Perhaps U.S. influence is greatest in the political realm. The United States has been responsible in recent years for setting up as well as for undermining a number of Dominican governments. Strong U.S. support at times bolstered Dominican governments and enabled them to survive; while U.S. opposition or sometimes only the withdrawal of such support caused other governments to collapse. Some AID officials have even begun sitting in at cabinet meetings. Supported by a great deal of evidence, close observers of the Dominican scene argue that the

United States is the most important force not only in Dominican external relations but in her internal affairs as well.

While U.S. influence in the Dominican Republic has clearly been vast, it has also been remarkably consistent. Many critics maintain that U.S. policy toward the Dominican Republic has been inconsistent, seeming to fluctuate between supporting dictatorship and supporting democracy; between promoting social change and hindering it; between favoring constitutionalism and working closely with the usurpers of constitutional government; or between upholding inter-American covenants and ignoring them. In fact, however, United States policy has for a long time been based on two rather constant principles: (1) the preservation and promotion of stability; and, concomitantly, (2) the prevention of a situation that could lead to the domination by a foreign power in a country that the United States considers to be strategically located and within its sphere of influence. In recent years, of course, this would mean the avoidance at all costs of a Communist or Castroist take-over.

Looking at U.S. policy toward the Dominican Republic with these principles in mind helps to explain the seeming vacillations of that policy in recent years. Because Trujillo provided stability, the United States backed the dictator for many years and began to oppose him only after 1959, when the Cuban example illustrated that brutal dictatorships provide good breeding grounds for Communism. After Trujillo's death, the United States consistently backed those elements in the Dominican Republic that seemed to provide the best hope for stability, continuity, and anti-Communism. The subsequent breakdown of stability and the fear that Communists were taking advantage of the chaos, by the same token, led the United States to intervene militarily in the Dominican Republic in 1965.

Although the preservation and promotion of stability and the prevention of Communism were the ultimate goals of the United States, differences in opinion may exist about the correct or most appropriate way for the United States to implement these policies in a given situation. Stability means different things to different people. Furthermore, stability in the short run—which dictatorial and unpopular governments often provide—may lead to chaos in the long run. Similarly, policy-makers have different notions about the best means to prevent Communism. Some U.S. officials prefer to work with strong-arm anti-Communist governments; others believe that the challenge of Communism should best be met by pushing democratic reforms and thereby eliminating the squalid and impoverished conditions of backwardness that cause Communism to grow. The Dominican Republic, indeed, provides an almost classic case where the Department of State, the CIA, the Pentagon, the labor attachés, and others were all facing in several different and often conflicting directions at once. On a number of occasions, there was no unified direction in U.S. policy toward the country, and the many U.S. organizations active in Dominican affairs frequently worked at cross purposes. These conflicts have not always resulted in the best interests of either the Dominican Republic or the United States being served. Indeed, some critics have argued that the principles on which U.S. policy operates are based on wrong or unenlightened assumptions and preconceptions about the modernization process in countries like the Dominican Republic and that U.S. policies and programs have often frustrated rather than encouraged Dominican national development.

While U.S. influence in the Dominican Republic's affairs is enormous, it is, paradoxically, also limited. The failure, for example, of some of the United States' top-priority aid programs despite enormous efforts illustrated the limits of the United States' power to effect change. Furthermore, the United States could not always convince a sovereign Dominican government to adopt a policy to which it was manifestly opposed or which it saw in a different light. Finally, the fact that the United States was so large and powerful and the Dominican Republic so small and weak often served as a restraint on U.S. activities. U.S. officials were frequently hesitant, because of their own orientations as well as because of world public opinion, to ride roughshod over Dominican feelings and sensitivities. Despite these limitations, however, the Dominican Republic remains in many ways a dependency of the United States.

Dominican political leaders, it must also be noted, frequently reverse the process by using the U.S. Embassy for their own purposes. Dominican politicians, for example, often go to considerable lengths to have their picture taken with the U.S. ambassador or with other embassy officials and have it appear in the press. Such pictures obviously have political implications both for the United States and the Dominican politicians involved. When making nationalistic appeals, furthermore, Dominicans may fulminate against the real or imagined policies of the U.S. Embassy. There is a whole host of techniques and procedures that Dominican *políticos* employ to use the power and influence of the United States for partisan or political advantage.

Though the U.S. is by far the most important country with which the Dominican Republic must deal, it maintains relations with many other nations and international organizations. It is a member of the United Nations and of the Organization of American States. It receives aid from several international lending institutions and is a signatory to several hemispheric defense pacts. The Dominican Republic is not as yet a member of a regional trade bloc.

Relations between the Dominican Republic and neighboring Haiti, which share the island of Hispaniola, have traditionally been strained. Dominicans are fond of pointing to the purity of their European traditions and tend to look down on what they consider the primitive and uncivilized Haitians. The Dominicans still talk of the Haitian invasions of the nineteenth century and of the barbarism and cruelty of the invaders. At the present time, the Dominican Republic is more powerful than Haiti and therefore takes pleasure in taunting and sometimes threatening the former French slave colony. Haiti is also used as a kind of national scapegoat; conflicts with Haiti are sometimes employed to stir nationalistic sentiment in the Dominican Republic, and international episodes are sometimes exaggerated to divert attention from pressing domestic problems. Fear of Haiti has helped shape Dominican political behavior for nearly two centuries.

Despite common Hispanic traditions, the Dominican Republic does not maintain particularly close relations with other states of the Western Hemisphere. Relations with nearby Puerto Rico, where many Dominicans have business connections or go for holidays, and with Venezuela, like Puerto Rico connected by direct air flights, are probably the closest. During the 1940's and 1950's, the many international conspiracies constantly brewing in the Caribbean and in Central America meant that the Dominican Republic kept close tabs on events in the entire area. More recently, however, as the region's international relations have become more stable, the Dominican Republic's contacts with Panama, Costa Rica, Nicaragua, Honduras, Guatemala, El Salvador, and Mexico have become more limited. The country of course maintains formal relations with the other Latin American nations, but the remoteness of the South American continent limits direct contacts.

Formal relations are also maintained with the West European nations. With the smaller of these—such as Denmark or Holland—the Dominican Republic has little contact and hence no need for a large mission. Diplomatic relations, thus, are frequently handled by a single representative who usually has business connections in the country, and whose position is mostly honorary. Larger embassy staffs are maintained in Great Britain, France, West Germany, and Spain, with whom the Dominican Republic maintains some tourist interchange and with whom it would like to increase its trade. An exchange of diplomats has also taken place with the Vatican, and the Papal nuncio in Santo Domingo has great influence on domestic Dominican politics.

The Dominican Republic's relations with the "third world" emerging nations in the Middle East, in South and Southeast Asia, and in Africa have thus far been extremely limited. By contrast, contact with Israel has increased: Israel is considered a model for economic development, and the vigorous personal efforts of the Israeli ambassador in Santo Domingo in promoting better relations between the two countries have had effect. (In 1967, this ambassador became embroiled in an unseemly public controversy about the Arab-Israel war and was replaced.) Trade, together with the presence of a large Chinese colony in the Dominican Republic, helps account for the considerable contacts maintained with Formosa. Some commerce is also carried out with Japan.

Hardly any contacts, official or unofficial, exist with the Communist nations—that is, with China, the Soviet Union, the East European countries, and Cuba. Although there has been some talk —as yet not widespread—of negotiating commercial arrangements with some Communist nations, none of them have accredited missions in Santo Domingo. A few Dominican Communists have traveled to and been trained in Cuba, Czechoslovakia, or the Soviet Union; sometimes they have managed to return to the Dominican Republic. But the Communists have so far not been a strong political force.

Though contacts with the Communist nations have been exceedingly limited and though the domestic extreme-left groups have traditionally been weak, disunited, inept, without charismatic leadership, and without popular support, Communism in the Dominican Republic is a subject that must be considered. First, the extreme leftist elements engage in extensive propaganda activities that are out of proportion to their actual strength. (The large number of anti-American and Communist slogans painted on walls and buildings have sometimes been mistakenly used by U.S. visitors as an index of Communist strength in the Dominican Republic. In fact, a very few people can be hired cheaply to "paint" the entire downtown area in one night.) Secondly and more importantly, "Communism" as an issue in Dominican politics is very important. Trujillo, initially, and later right-wing politicians, clerics, and military officers learned to manipulate the issues of "Communism" and "Communist infiltration" with proficiency both for domestic and U.S. consumption. Although the charges are usually highly exaggerated or completely trumped up, the cry of "Communism!" strikes a responsive chord in certain quarters.

In a sense, both the enormous influence of the U.S. in so many major aspects of Dominican life and the role that Communists and the issue of "Communism" play in the Dominican Republic have been equally unfortunate. For despite the many benefits that U.S. assistance has brought to the country, a side effect has been the introduction of a highly divisive but, for the Dominican Republic, largely extraneous and irrelevant issue—the Cold War—into domestic Dominican affairs at a time when the nation could hardly afford another source of severe political discord. It was largely the issue of Communism and the perceived threat of a potential Communist take-over that led to Bosch's overthrow in 1963 and that during the 1965 revolution prompted United States military intervention—with all the bitter and highly disruptive political repercussions that these events precipitated.

These comments are not meant to imply that the tensions and hostilities generated in the Dominican Republic over a long period of time would not have occurred without the introduction of Cold War issues. It is to say, however, that the divisions and antagonisms already existing in the country were further aggravated by the Cold War conflicts and that these conflicts greatly complicated the Dominican Republic's attempt to bridge the transition from the dictatorship of Trujillo to a more democratic political system. The already difficult process of nation-building and modernization in the Dominican Republic was made even more difficult by the intrusion of still one more major source of deep and bitter conflict in a society already torn by seemingly irreconcilable divisions.

Chapter XIII

CONCLUSION

THE DOMINICAN REPUBLIC, like many Asian, African, and other Latin American nations, has in recent years experienced the rapid acceleration of the process of development and modernization. The traditional, agrarian-based, two-class, *caudillo*- and "first family"-dominated, semi-feudal structure has begun to give way as the country has developed economically, as new social groups and newer forms of organizations have emerged, and as new ideas concerning the way the economy, the society, and the polity should be structured have become more widespread. The sweep and scope of the broadscale changes currently taking place are revolutionary in their magnitude and portent; the Dominican Republic is being fundamentally transformed from top to bottom and in every area and sector of national life.

The tensions, immense problems and difficulties, instability, and revolutionary upheavals which the country has experienced in the contemporary period are largely a reflection of the transition from underdeveloped to developed, and of the conflict between old and new, between traditional and modern. While the Dominican Republic has been changing at an accelerated speed in recent years, it still has a decidedly mixed system—neither wholly traditional nor wholly modern but a complex, often confusing, certainly unstable, and frequently chaotic jumble of the two. It remains for us in this chapter to summarize in the light of this overriding theme what has been said before and to offer some conclusions concerning the process of development and modernization in the Dominican Republic.

Geographically, we have stated, Hispaniola's strategic location has long made it subject to foreign control and direction. In this century, the United States, which feels that the entire Caribbean area is of fundamental strategic importance to its security, has been the power most concerned with preserving in the Dominican Republic a stable government, friendly to its interests. In 1965, the United States did not consider that its interests would be served by the restoration of Bosch to the presidency, and even though the restoration of democratic government was favored by most Dominicans, the United States intervened militarily to prevent the Constitutionalist revolution from succeeding. It was felt that Bosch's return might lead to a Castro-like take-over. The overwhelming presence in Dominican affairs of the "Colossus of the North," concerned primarily, after all, with promoting its own interests and not necessarily those of its weak neighbor, has further complicated the development process in the Dominican Republic. At the present time, therefore, the Dominican Republic cannot modernize in its own way, on its own terms, because it is inevitably drawn into Cold War conflicts which are often only of peripheral importance to it. These conflicts have resulted in the interjection of a variety of divisive but essentially tangential issues into an already severely divided country and made the process of national development even more difficult.

The physiography of the Dominican Republic, with its high mountains and inadequate communication and transportation networks, has until recently perpetuated and reinforced regionalism and localism, and has prevented the growth of a modern, centralized state. When a centralized state was finally established, it took the form of Trujillo's cruel dictatorship. The expanding communication and transportation systems were a mixed blessing since they enabled Trujillo to exercise even more absolute control over the nation. Only in the past few years has the network of roads and communications been put to use to help promote national development and democratic growth.

The Dominican Republic is a country of considerable natural wealth, but this wealth has not greatly benefited the bulk of the population. Most of the wealth has always drained away to foreign accounts or into private pockets. Only in recent years has the natural wealth of the country been exploited more efficiently and with some concern for the welfare of all Dominicans and not just a favored few. Today, more and more Dominicans are demanding a greater share of the national patrimony and of the wealth traditionally belonging to the small Dominican elite, and it is clear that the legitimate demands of the people must soon be met if another bloody revolution shall be avoided.

Historically, the Dominican Republic experienced much of the worst of Spain's colonial heritage: an authoritarian, hierarchical, rigid, absolutist, and closed system that provided few possibilities for change or gradual growth. The country's history after independence was characterized by a rapid changeover of presidents, constitutions, and governments; by alternating periods of extreme dictatorship and extreme chaos; by a succession of foreign pressures and occupations; and by seemingly insoluble social and economic problems. At the start of the 1960's the country had had practically no experience with the institutions and practices of democratic government—or, indeed, with any functioning, viable system. The attempt to establish democracy in the post-Trujillo period was not very successful in large measure because few Dominicans knew what democracy meant or understood and accepted the preconditions on which democracy could be built.

The people of the Dominican Republic are friendly, gentle, dignified, and long-suffering. Furthermore, they share the same religious, linguistic, and cultural background. But friendliness and certain uniformities have not led to the development of a unified and integrated society. The Dominicans share a growing sense of nationalism and the awareness of being Dominican, but they agree on little else. The values which are a part of the Dominican "political culture"—extreme individualism, personalism, etc.—have worked, in fact, to prevent the growth of a spirit of compromise and conciliation, the building of consensus, and the emphasis on community which are necessary if a political system is to remain reasonably stable and democratic.

The Dominican Republic has traditionally had an essentially two-class social structure composed of a small group at the top, a large number at the bottom, and relatively few in between. Class lines have always been tightly drawn, and the different sectors maintained wholly different life-styles as well. Though social change and the possibilities for social mobility are now increasing, divisions within and between the social groups and classes remain deep and have become more bitter. The traditional groups cling tenaciously to their wealth, power, and special privileges, refusing to share them with the rising labor, peasant, and middle sectors. At the same time the emerging forces, frustrated by the unwillingness of the few to permit the growth of a more equitable and just society by gradual, evolutionary means, inevitably turn to radical, violent solutions. The Dominican Republic has become an increasingly polarized nation—rich versus poor, privileged versus underprivileged, oligarchy versus the people, powerful versus powerless—which has made any moderate middle-of-the-road solution to the nation's pressing problems all but impossible.

Nor has the Dominican educational system provided the necessary instruction and training to enable the country to modernize. From the grade schools to the universities, the Dominican Republic is beset by a variety of difficulties that prevent the growth of a literate, skilled, and educated population. Similarly, Dominican culture has not provided the cement necessary to rally the country around common and well-known themes and traditions, thus helping to hold the nation together.

Economically, the Dominican Republic is still a very poor and underdeveloped country. The per capita income of most Dominicans is next to nothing. Overwhelming reliance on the production of a single crop to sell on the world market has made the entire economy—and hence the government itself—subject to the vagaries of that market. The country is caught in a series of interlocking social, economic, and political vicious circles which seem impossible to break. In the meantime poverty, want, misery, starvation, and hopelessness persist.

The Dominican Republic's political problems are perhaps paramount. If the country had a popular and effective government which could carry out the sorely needed reforms, it could begin to live up to its potential. But such a government has not yet come to power in the Dominican Republic—indeed, the nature of Dominican social and political realities make it a near impossibility. On the one hand reform-minded governments, such as that of Bosch, cannot hope to remain in power in the face of the concerted opposition of the Dominican establishment. And on the other hand, the governments that were acceptable to the traditional sectors, such as the Council of State and the Reid regime, have not been interested in or oriented toward carrying out basic reforms. A government like Balaguer's, which attempts to appease the elite groups and at the same time to promote limited reforms, must be prepared to face the vicious and sometimes concerted opposition of both the powerful extreme right and the left.

The political dilemmas go deeper than this, however. The Dominican Republic's laws and legal system, its constitutional system and the formal structure of government, and its bureaucratic organization often have little to do with the way the system actually works. Government institutions and the formal-legal rules of procedure do not always accurately reflect Dominican political realities and seem to have little relevance to the lives of most Dominicans. Furthermore, the political parties and interest associations are not adequately performing their functions. Dominican public policies have most often been inefficient, chaotic, discontinuous, and hence unsuccessful, having little effect on the very persons they were designed to benefit. The entire political system of the Dominican Republic seems to be dysfunctional—and dysfunctional with a vengeance.

In almost every area of national life, then—geographical, historical, behavioral, social, educational, cultural, economic, and political—the Dominican Republic faces enormous problems and dilemmas that prevent the country's rapid development. Since all these aspects are intrinsically interrelated, since change and development (or decay and disintegration) in one sphere must inevitably have repercussions in others, we are led to conclude that the over-all problems of modernization and development must also be viewed in an all-encompassing and interrelated manner. It is thus practically impossible to separate political from social and economic development. In the Dominican Republic, the dilemmas of development are mutually reinforcing; the vicious circles really do interlock. Viewed in this light the prospects for Dominican development—at least in the short run—do not at all appear promising, for the basic social, economic, and political infrastructure on which a more modern system could be built is largely nonexistent.

Prior to Trujillo's coming to power in 1930, the Dominican Republic was essentially a traditional, semi-feudal land. The earliest stages of industrialization had hardly begun, and the communications and transportation systems were undeveloped. The society was divided into two widely separated classes and was governed by semi-feudal arrangements of land ownership, serfdom, and peonage. Modern kinds of organizations—political parties, a bureaucracy, a professional armed force, or associational interest groups—were nonexistent or in their infancy. Control of the government was most often determined by competing men on horseback, often in alliance with rival first families, who sought to muster enough strength to take power.

The long Trujillo dictatorship, 1930–61, was cruel, bloody, and oppressive, but it also marked a watershed in Dominican history. However undemocratic, Trujillo's regime marked the beginning of the transition to modernity; the country can no longer go back to the kind of semi-feudal order that existed prior to 1930. During the Trujillo era, roads were built and the entire country opened up and its governmental system centralized. The armed forces and the public service were also greatly expanded, made more efficient, and centralized. New social sectors, such as labor and the middle classes, began to emerge and grow as a result of industrialization and the over-all economic growth that occurred. The entire population began to become aware of new ideological currents, and the structure of society grew more complex. While many of these changes were a part of the modernization process, in the Dominican Republic they also provided the basis for increasingly dictatorial control. Trujillo greatly improved the communications system and the armed forces, for example, but these improvements were designed to strengthen his dictatorship, and they did not promote national growth. By such means Trujillo not only destroyed much of the country's old order, but the newer more modernizing groups and organizations that had begun to emerge were also methodically snuffed out or subjected to the dictator's control.

The Trujillo dictatorship, with its increasingly more totalitarian-like system of controls, bequeathed to the Dominican Republic a legacy which rendered the rebuilding of the nation —socially, economically, morally, politically—almost impossible. Practically none of the minimum requirements for a functioning viable system—be it democratic or any other kind—were present in the post-Trujillo Dominican Republic. The nature of Trujillo's extremely personal and increasingly totalitarian control meant that upon the death of the dictator, no group, individual, or institution could begin to fill the void. During a period in which much of Latin America was beginning to develop or accelerating the development of more modern and more democratic systems, the Dominican Republic experienced only a perverted kind of development that fed the bank accounts and the megalomania of one man. Trujillo's rule thus left a deeply ingrained, all-pervasive negative heritage of hate, terror, corruption, and ruin, which made the prospects for democratic development in the post-Trujillo period difficult at best.

While Trujillo's rule had been characterized by absolute monolithic control over all aspects of Dominican life, the period after his death was marked by the frenetic, tumultuous, untrammeled, and frequently chaotic activities of a society emerging from the dark despair of thirty-one years of dictatorship. The demand for the benefits of modern life quickly outran the ability of the government to satisfy these demands, and frustration soon set in. Economic growth occurred, but few of the benefits trickled down. The gap between rich and poor widened.

Most Dominicans assumed that the overthrow of the Trujillos would surely and immediately usher in a new and better era of prosperity and well-being. But the modernization and reform of an entire society cannot be achieved overnight, as both the Dominicans and the many U.S. assistance missions soon sadly learned. The Dominican Republic's experiment with building a model of democracy on the heels of the overthrow of an extremely oppressive dictatorship failed, and it failed miserably. Failure, bitter disappointment, and deep disillusionment also fanned the flames of revolutionary sentiments.

The Dominican Republic remains a highly divided and fragmented society. The various sectors active in national life—the military, the Church, the several business, professional, and landowning elites, the labor movement, the peasantry, the political parties—are not only unable to cooperate in the establishment of a viable political system, but they also share no common basis of understanding or communication. The gaps between rich and poor and between the vested and the newly rising forces are still too wide for the country to become an integrated nation. Rather, politics in the Dominican Republic resembles a group of warring sub-nations or, to mix the metaphor, a system of centrifugal forces, each spinning in a different orbit, with little attachment to a central nucleus, and tending to fly apart. It is thus not surprising that the entire system is prone to serious and recurrent breakdowns.

Most of the population—especially the lower class but also some of the middle class elements—have no say in national affairs. When Bosch attempted to govern for and in the name of these traditionally forgotten and downtrodden elements, he was quickly overthrown. Yet the downtrodden are no longer content to remain in that miserable condition and rose up in 1965 in a bloody, hate-filled protest. The dilemma of Dominican politics is that a progressive and reform-oriented government cannot survive in the face of opposition from the powerful Dominican elite, the military, and the Church hierarchy; that a right-wing or conservative regime cannot last in the face of rising revolutionary pressures; and that no strong moderate middle way has as yet evolved.

The Dominican Republic lacks most of the fundamental prerequisites for a stable and effective political system. Its educational and value system, and its economy and social structure are just not conducive to the development of the modern, democratic nation that almost all Dominicans desire. The best evidence for the correctness of this assertion is the almost total breakdown of the system in 1965 into revolution, civil war, and chaos.

Even before the 1965 upheaval and the subsequent United States intervention, then, deep and perhaps irreconcilable divisions existed within the nation. There was no parity or equilibrium or system of checks and balances. In fact, the society and political system were highly imbalanced and in disequilibrium with certain sectors, such as the military and the wealthy elite, having an overwhelming preponderance of power. The society was stratified horizontally in a rigid class system and vertically in an equally rigid system of warring factions. Several successive governments were considered illegitimate by large blocs of the population, and practically no consensus existed concerning the ends or means of national policy.

If Dominican society and politics were highly divided, imbalanced, and unintegrated before the 1965 revolution, they have become even more so since that time. For what the revolution, civil war, and U.S. intervention did was to tear apart whatever there was of political and social solidarity in the country and to polarize an already deeply divided country even more severely. The discord and antagonisms that existed prior to the revolution became bitter hatreds and open, festering sores, which neither the traditional affability of the Dominicans nor the inauguration of a newly-elected constitutional government in 1966 can readily gloss over.

Surface tranquility barely hides the disintegration of the nation. The atmosphere of terror persists, and, as in the dark days of Trujillo, those opposed to the government or to the military are frequently beaten and sometimes "disappear" without leaving a trace. Disputes which can be resolved in other systems with a minimum of conflict are still frequently disputed in violent clashes in the Dominican Republic. The social and political fabric of the nation has disintegrated, and the slim threads that hold the country together are weak, over-extended, and ready to snap at any time.

In the absence of stable institutions and a functioning political system, Dominican politics tends to be extremely unstable, chaotic, and violence-prone. Political life is thus characterized by the naked and frequently brutal pursuit, display, and exercise of power, unrefined by such moderating influences as a strong party system, an effective Congress or bureaucracy, or many well-balanced interest associations. At least at this particular time in the nation's development, Dominican politics must be approached from the point of view that turbulence, force, upheaval, chaos, violence, revolution, and institutional discontinuity are normal and to be expected, while stability, continuity, and peaceful, gradual, and evolutionary change are abnormal and unlikely.

The Dominican political system undoubtedly benefited from the interim regime of President Héctor García Godoy and the subsequent elected government of Balaguer. But the larger issues, which the revolution tragically and unmistakably brought to the surface, have so far not been solved or even adequately faced up to. They relate to such problems as the role of an oppressive and widely hated military, the enormous differences between rich and poor, the question of dictatorship versus democracy, the great need for social and economic reform, the desire of the Dominicans for control over their own destinies without foreign influence, and the role of the United States and the Communists in Dominican affairs.

The provisional presidency of García Godoy weathered an at times stormy interim period and muted some severe conflicts— no mean accomplishment in the rocky Dominican political system. The relatively simple expedients of the withdrawal of foreign troops, the holding of elections, the inauguration of Balaguer's government, the enactment of a new constitution, and the promotion of more moderate and conciliatory policies on the part of the Balaguer administration are all laudable also. But these accomplishments should not disguise the severe, long-term damage that the social and political system has suffered. The dispatch of U.S. troops and their interposition between the contending Dominican forces represented an interruption of the 1965 revolution but not its resolution. Until the basic wants and demands of the outwardly friendly and peaceable but inwardly bitter and resentful bulk of the Dominican population are met, the country is liable to explode again, this time, however, in a revolution far more violent and probably far more anti-United States than occurred in 1965.

The Dominican Republic has begun the great leap from a traditional, backward, semi-feudal system into the modern, industrialized twentieth century world; it is, we have said, in the process of transition from underdeveloped to developed. At the present time, however, it is neither the one nor the other; it has modernized in some respects but remains traditional in others and mixed or transitional in a hodge-podge variety of ways. The country is thus torn between old and new, between traditional and modern; and the many conflicts stemming from these divisions have so far proved irreconcilable. While much the same could be said of many other developing nations, the extreme combination of all these divisive and disruptive tendencies and their extreme degree help to make the Dominican system unique and account for its having come apart at the seams and very nearly completely unraveled. It is unlikely, given these conditions, that a viable, functioning, and effective democratic system will soon or easily be established in the Dominican Republic.

It is difficult to avoid a pessimistic conclusion concerning the prospects for democratic development and modernization in the Dominican Republic—at least for the foreseeable future. For those who in recent years have worked in and have come to love and care for this beautiful but tragic country and its friendly personable people, the apparent hopelessness of the immense problems and the often futile attempts to try to solve them evoke a sad but common lament: "Poor D.R." Among those who with feeling and genuine dedication have studied or labored long and hard on Dominican problems and dilemmas, the shared realization seems to grow that a kind of national malaise—fate, unfavorable circumstances, and sheer bad luck—is working against the country's chances of ever becoming a modern nation. For whenever it appeared that the Dominican Republic was beginning to overcome its past difficulties, something always seemed to happen that frustrated not only the particular program at issue or the government in power at the time but dashed all hope as well.

The Dominican Republic is not altogether unique in these regards, for we know from experience and from other studies of political development that instability, inefficiency, chaos, and upheaval frequently accompany the transitional process. Yet from the human point of view of the people involved, it is painfully discouraging when plans go awry for no apparent logical reason, when few programs seem to work right or as anticipated, or when the long and painstaking efforts of many individuals over many years are destroyed overnight. To those others who have arrived at a similar pessimistic conclusion, this writer can only echo the thought that almost daily occurred to him while living and working in the country: "Poor people, poor D. R."

SUGGESTIONS FOR FURTHER READING

BOSCH, JUAN. *The Unfinished Experiment: Democracy in the Dominican Republic.* New York: Frederick A. Praeger, 1965. The former president's account of the post-Trujillo period and his own term in office.

———. *Trujillo: Causas de una tiranía sin ejemplo.* Caracas: Grabados Nacionales, 1959. Attempts to explain Trujillo's regime psychologically by examining the Dominican socio-economic background.

CLARK, JAMES A. *The Church and the Crisis in the Dominican Republic.* Westminster, Md.: The Newman Press, 1967. A first-hand account of the 1965 events by an American priest who is highly sympathetic to the Church.

CRASSWELLER, ROBERT D. *Trujillo: The Life and Times of a Caribbean Dictator.* New York: Macmillan, 1966. An excellent and well-written historical study.

Dominican Action 1965: Intervention or Cooperation? Washington, D.C.: Georgetown University, Center for Strategic Studies, 1966. Contains previously unpublished information about the revolution made available to the authors by the Johnson administration.

ESPAILLAT, ARTURO. *Trujillo: The Last Caesar.* Chicago: Henry Regnery, 1963. A colorful and, at times, hard-to-believe account, by Trujillo's intelligence chief.

GALINDEZ, JESUS DE. *La era de Trujillo.* Santiago de Chile: Editorial del Pacífico, 1956. The first scholarly full-length study of the Trujillo regime—for which its author was killed.

Jimenez-Grullon, Juan Isidro. *La República Dominicana: Una ficción.* Mérida, Venezuela: Talleres Gráficos Universitarios, 1965. Socio-politico-economic survey of the Dominican Republic past and present.

Kurzman, Dan. *Santo Domingo: Revolt of the Damned.* New York: G. P. Putnam's Sons, 1965. Critical account of U.S. actions during the 1965 revolution by a reporter for *The Washington Post.*

Logan, Rayford W. *Haiti and the Dominican Republic.* New York: Oxford University Press, 1968. An historical account of the two countries on Hispaniola with some effort at comparison.

Mallin, Jay. *Caribbean Crisis: Subversion Fails in the Dominican Republic.* New York: Doubleday, 1965. Commissioned by the U.S. government and sympathetic to U.S. actions during the 1965 revolution.

Martin, John Bartlow. *Overtaken by Events: The Dominican Crisis from the Fall of Trujillo to the Civil War.* New York: Doubleday, 1966. Interesting account by the former U.S. Ambassador to the Dominican Republic.

Ornes, German. *Trujillo: Little Caesar of the Caribbean.* New York: Nelson, 1958. Among the best and most complete accounts of the Trujillo regime, by a Dominican newspaper editor.

Roberts, T. D. *Area Handbook for the Dominican Republic.* Washington, D.C.: American University, Foreign Area Studies, 1966. A comprehensive compilation of basic facts about the political, economic, social, and military practices and institutions of the Dominican Republic.

Rodman, Selden. *Quisqueya: A History of the Dominican Republic.* Seattle, Wash.: University of Washington Press, 1964. A brief and readable history.

Szulc, Tad. *Dominican Diary.* New York: Delacorte Press, 1965. Critical account of the 1965 U.S. intervention by a reporter for *The New York Times.*

Welles, Sumner. *Naboth's Vineyard: The Dominican Republic, 1844–1924.* New York: Payson and Clarke, 1928. A classic history of the Dominican Republic prior to the Trujillo period by the former U.S. Assistant Secretary of State for Latin American Affairs.

Wiarda, Howard J. *Dictatorship and Development: The Methods of Control in Trujillo's Dominican Republic.* Gainesville, Florida:

University of Florida Press, 1968. Places the Trujillo regime in historical and comparative perspective.

——— (ed.). *Dominican Republic: Election Factbook.* Washington, D.C.: Institute for the Comparative Study of Political Systems, 1966. Information on parties, candidates, electoral system, issues, voting.

———. *Materials for the Study of Politics and Government in the Dominican Republic, 1930–1966.* Santiago de los Caballeros: Universidad Católica "Madre y Maestra," 1968. Bibliography and introductory note on research environment and research facilities in the Dominican Republic.

INDEX